WHAT NOBODY EVER TOLD US

A Guide to Getting More Out of the Catholic Mass

Philip A. Smith

Understand the Mass Press

Understand the Mass Press. Sylvania, Ohio (USA).

ISBN: 9798729360826 (paperback)

Printed in the United States of America.

RESCRIPT

In accord with canons 824 and 827 §3 of the *Codex Iuris Canonici*, the undersigned hereby grants permission to publish *What Nobody Ever Told Us: A Guide to Getting More Out of the Catholic Mass*, by Reverend Philip Smith.

The permission to publish the above-named work is valid for the original text but not for new editions or translation of the same (c.f. canon 829).

Notice of this rescript is to be printed on the reverse side of the title page of the book.

Given at the Chancery in the Diocese of Toledo in America on the fourth day of December, in the year of our Lord, two thousand twenty.

Most Reverend Daniel E. Thomas
Bishop of Toledo

Sister Rose Marie Timmer, RSM
Chancellor

CONTENTS

INTRODUCTION

How can I get more out of the Mass?

I will never forget the day during freshman religion class when Jonathan raised his hand and blurted out what most of the class had been thinking. Our religion teacher was lecturing about the Catholic requirement of attending Mass every Sunday. Jonathan spoke up and said: "Mass is so boring! I don't get anything out of it."

The teacher paused, obviously and considerably frustrated. Yet, the fact that several high schoolers lifted their bored heads off their desks made it clear that Jonathan's statement struck a chord. The teacher realized that Jonathan had given him an opportunity to engage pupils who were typically apathetic towards his material.

Walking with a swagger of purposefulness towards the dusty blackboard, the teacher picked up a short piece of yellow chalk and wrote a three-digit number on the board. Pointing to the number, he asked the class: "Do you know what this number represents?"

The room was silent.

Slowly, he tapped the chalk against the board as the teenagers stared with blank looks at the number 168.

The instructor paused further for dramatic effect.

Then he finally gave the answer. "There are 168 hours in every week."

Restlessness spread in the room. Where was the teacher going with this lesson? One or two students returned their heads to a resting position of apathy on their desks.

Quickly, the teacher posed a question: "How much time does Sunday Mass take out of your week?"

One of the few students who actually attended Sunday Mass supplied the answer: "60 minutes".

Then the teacher launched into his argument: "God gives you 168 hours per week and all God asks from you is one hour per week at church. Sixty minutes! Don't you think you could spend one hour per week at Mass out of gratitude for all God has done for you?"

The room was still as the teacher looked over at Jonathan who replied quickly: "That doesn't change much. The Mass is still boring. I still don't get anything out of it."

Smiling, the teacher recited what is perhaps the most frequently employed Catholic guilt trip to encourage Mass attendance: "Jonathan, you will never get more out of the Mass until you put more into the Mass."

Then the teacher returned to his lecture.

Twelve years later I was standing in front of a classroom of Catholic university students teaching Introduction to Catholicism and I found myself regurgitating the same arguments my high school religion teacher had employed. One of my students had been arguing that the Catholic Mass was boring, in fact, *very* boring, compared to the new church she had been attending with her boyfriend. The music at the new church was contemporary and upbeat. The pastor was young and trendy. The environment was casual. They even served coffee. *Free* coffee.

The student quipped that she did not think she would ever enjoy Mass again after such a fun and lively worship experience.

I thought I had a good answer for her. But, in reality, I did not. I employed the two arguments that Catholics usually put forward in this situation. Her reaction, followed by comments from other students, quickly confirmed that my arguments were not convincing. Their candid criticism led me to do some deep soul-searching as I drove home from campus that cold February evening. I had to face the fact that these two common arguments were not only unpersuasive, but also theologically problematic.

The first argument goes like this: "Sure, attending Mass might be painful and boring for you, but you need to put up with it to show your gratitude to God." The guilt trip reaches its crescendos with the famous line: "Remember, Jesus suffered for you for three long hours on a cross...the least you can do for him is to go to Mass one hour per week."

This answer is unsatisfactory because the Catholic Church teaches that the Mass is the deepest encounter with God possible on earth. Encountering the Almighty, Awesome God of the universe should not just be an hour of drudgery we suffer through as a glorified thank-you card for what God has done for us.

The second classic response to complaints about the Mass sounds like this: "The reason why Mass is so boring for you is that you are not trying hard enough. You need to put more into the Mass, and then you will get more out of the Mass!"

This answer also is unsatisfactory. It assumes our efforts are more important than what God does at the Mass. Secondly, most of us have no idea of how to "try harder", no idea of how we can really put more "effort" into the Mass. No one has ever taught us how to pray at Mass, or what to do at the Mass.

As I drove my aging, white Ford SUV down pothole-ridden Douglas Road that dark and crisp winter evening after class, I realized that this was a major problem in the Catholic Church. Not just for my students in Toledo, but for Catholics of all ages. Most Catholics have only learned what *not* to do at the Mass.

People taught us not to talk out loud. Not to chew gum. Not to run inside the church and not to stand up on the pews. Not to use our cell phones at Mass, either.

In other words, sit still, be quiet, and watch.

This is a major tragedy! Simply put, good-intentioned people trained us to be spectators at Mass. We were taught to watch the priest and other ministers attentively, as if we were watching some form of entertainment unfold before our eyes. No wonder we are bored at the Mass!

Once I arrived home, I sat down at my desk even though it was already late, and I started re-designing my teaching notes. I needed to teach the students what no one had taught them before. The Mass was always going to be boring to them unless someone explained what to do with their minds and hearts during each specific part of the Mass, what the purpose of these rituals were, how they could enter into them and encounter God. I had to show them how God uses the rituals of the Mass to work powerfully in our lives.

As I reflected on my own understanding of the Mass, it dawned on me for the first time that I was sitting in a privileged position. I had the blessing of several years studying theology at an undergraduate and graduate level. I learned much about the meaning of the Mass during those nine years. My graduate studies took place in the Eternal City of Rome, providing many unique experiences and encounters that further deepened my understanding of the Mass.

I was passionate about the Mass, loved participating in the Mass, and got so much out of the Mass because I had actually been taught the meaning of the Mass in great detail. Recognizing that this formation is tragically foreign to most Catholics, I knew I needed to share with others what I had learned about the Mass.

The next time I taught my university students about the Mass, I shared with them what I had learned during my years of theological study. I ditched the clichés and guilt trips from my previous lesson plans and taught them the meaning behind the words, gestures, and actions of the Mass. I shared anecdotes of how those truths had come alive during my participation in the Mass as my adult life unfolded.

The response was astounding. One student said it was the most amazing religion class he had ever attended. Another student said she wanted to find a Mass to attend that night to practice what she learned during class. A startling comment, since our night class concluded at 8:45 PM. There was even a student who was angry. He threw up his hands about half-way through the class and emphatically shouted: "Why didn't anyone tell me this before? If more people knew this, they would want to go to Mass every Sunday or every single day."

After class, he came to the front of the room and said: "Thank you for teaching us what nobody ever told us about the Mass."

Since that night, I have taught many more classes about the Mass to college students at the university. I have also travelled throughout my diocese giving presentations about the Mass for high school students, young adult retreats, adult education programs, and senior citizen gatherings.

The response has always been the same. People approached me afterwards and thanked me for sharing what nobody had ever told them before about how to pray at the Mass. There was so much they had been missing during the Mass.

My belief is that there is always "more" we can get out of the Mass. The purpose of this book is to help you discover this "more" in your own life. To help open up for you the meaning behind the words and gestures of the Catholic Mass so you can encounter God in the deepest way possible. Whether you are a cradle Catholic who has been attending Mass for decades, a recent convert to Catholicism who has just been attending for a few years, or someone who is not Catholic and has only attended Mass once or twice, this book will walk you through each prayer and ritual in the Mass and explain what should be the focus of your active participation in these moments. Most of all, this book will unpack what God is doing at each stage of the Mass and how we can cooperate with the grace God is offering us.

THE INTRODUCTORY
RITES

THE ENTRANCE

"Why you kiss table?"

During the time I served at a college campus, many non-Catholic students visited our church and attended Mass. An especially large group arrived near the end of each semester to complete an assignment for their World Religions class. The professor required students to attend a religious service at a church in the area and write a paper about it. Our church was always a popular choice, conveniently located across the street from campus.

One afternoon during Mass, I noticed two students diligently scribbling in their notebooks. Afterward, they approached and requested a few minutes to ask some questions. The two young women were international students from Vietnam. This was their first time in a Catholic Church building and first time attending a Catholic Mass.

It all seemed very strange to them and their first question was: "Why you kiss table?"

I paused, noticing their look of deep confusion, and I was unsure of what that meant: "Why you kiss table?"

The student assumed I could not understand her thick accent, so pointing at the altar, she repeated: "Why you kiss table?"

I realized the student was asking why the priest kisses the altar when he enters the sanctuary at the beginning of the Mass. She had a good reason to be perplexed and even disgusted by that gesture. After all, when was the last time anyone you know kissed a table?

So, why does the priest kiss the altar as one of the first ritual acts of the Mass?

The meaning of a kiss in Western culture can help us understand what is happening at the beginning of the Mass. A kiss typically expresses closeness and esteem between persons who have entered into a relationship. For example, parents kiss their children to show love and affection for them. A husband uses a kiss to show his esteem for his wife. The gesture expresses closeness, communion, and intimacy between two people, while also indicating a desire for greater closeness, communion, and intimacy between them.

At Mass, a kiss takes on similar meaning as the priest kisses the altar to indicate that a relationship characterized by love, esteem, and affection will unfold at the altar. Something very intimate, special, and deeply personal will happen there. We will experience God there! At the Lord's Table, we will experience how God desperately wants to be near to us and have a significant relationship with us.

God put aside his divine majesty and became one of us, to draw sinful humanity back to himself. God's plan to prove his love for us included dying on a cross as a sacrifice – an act of love. This act of love is what we remember when the priest reverences the altar with a kiss. We recall Jesus on Calvary giving of himself – totally and entirely – to convince us of his desire to have a relationship with us. The altar in the sanctuary of a church evokes the question: How will I respond to Jesus' gift of himself? He has sacrificed his life for me. How will I respond?

Through the ritual of the Mass, we give our answer to these questions. We accept Jesus' offer of friendship, allowing him to lead us in true worship.

In fact, even before the priest arrives at the altar something else occurs – and it does not initially make the most sense.

Have you ever wondered why we begin Mass with a procession?

Why don't the priest and altar servers just go to their seats 5 or 10 minutes before Mass to get settled and reflect for a few minutes like everyone else?

Why do we give children (altar servers) a large, heavy cross and lit torches to carry in procession while wearing long robes that they could easily trip over as they climb steep steps into the sanctuary of the church? Sometimes we even give them a pot of burning incense to carry up the aisle.

Talk about a safety hazard! Of course, the same could be said for others in the procession: usually a lector with a big, heavy book and a priest with a couple layers of robes (vestments) that could cause even the most physically fit person to trip as he walks, climb steps, and sings all at the same time.

Why don't we just simplify things and start Mass in a way that involves less movement?

The procession is a great visual reminder of what is taking place during the entire Mass. God is coming to his people. At the Mass, we experience Jesus who is Emmanuel, which means "God is with us", who takes the initiative to be with his people as they journey through life.

During the procession, the Book of the Gospels is carried as a sign that Jesus will speak inspiring words of truth and guidance to us during the Mass for our life journey. Candles in the procession are a sign that the light of Jesus will shine brightly to guide us through dark times of our journey. A crucifix in the procession reminds us we do not carry our crosses alone, but we follow after Jesus who carries our crosses with us and leads us to share in his victory over sin and death.

And, of course, the priest also walks in the procession. Jesus will use the words and the actions of the priest during the Mass to reassure us of his love for us as he says to us through the priest: "This is my body given for you...this is my blood shed for you...for the forgiveness of sins".

Our circumstances often change as life unfolds here on earth, but the procession at the beginning of the Mass reminds us that God journeys with us. The Mass is an encounter with the God who accompanies us and takes the initiative to love us, support us, teach us, challenge us, and lead us to heaven.

In fact, for several centuries in Rome, especially during Lent, the entire congregation would process through the streets of the neighborhood together before entering the church for Mass.

Their procession was a vivid reminder that the Christian life involves movement. The Christian life involves change. The Christian life involves allowing Jesus to push us out from where we are comfortable to live boldly the adventure of Christian service he has planned for us. God uses community on our journey to support us and help us grow.

The procession ultimately leads the priest to the altar, which points to the sacrificial dimension of the love Jesus expressed giving his life for us on the cross. The center area of the altar that the priest reverently kisses is usually the location of a small relic of a saint. This relic reminds us that the sacrificial love of Jesus we encounter at the Mass can empower us to live our own lives with saintly charity and enthusiasm. The divine love we encounter at the Mass takes us beyond our own human weaknesses, leading us to transcend typical human selfishness.

The beginning of Mass is a time for us to reflect on our own life journey. The Procession is a time to meditate on how God has been with us on our life journey during the past week. It is a time to give thanks that God is with us on our journey and to beg God to give us wisdom, guidance, and strength as we process into the future. This is the time to consider where God is leading us on our journey and how God is inviting us to reflect the sacrificial love of his Son, Jesus in our own lives.

THE SIGN OF THE CROSS

The Priest:
In the name of the Father, and of the Son, and of the
  Holy Spirit.
The people:
Amen.

When was the last time you made the Sign of the Cross and thought about the meaning of what you were doing?

I have to admit that the first time someone asked me this question, I did not have a very good response. I was caught. I could not remember the last time I had actually thought about it - even though it is a sign I make multiple times a day as a priest.

It is very easy to enter into auto-pilot mode when we make the Sign of the Cross.

From its earliest days, the Christian community has been making the Sign of the Cross. We are following in the footsteps of many centuries of Christians when we begin and end our prayers this way. It has also been a Christian custom to begin and end one's day by making the Sign of the Cross. Many important theologians in the early Church like St. Justin Martyr (just a hundred years or so after Jesus' death and resurrection), St. Jerome, St. Cyril of Jerusalem, St. Ambrose, and St. Augustine all taught about the powerful meaning behind this sign.

What does making the Sign of the Cross actually mean?

When we trace the cross on our bodies we are accepting God's love for us. We are acknowledging how much we are loved.

We trace the outline of the cross since it was the place where

Jesus proved his love for us in the most moving way possible. We trace on ourselves the outline of the cross where Jesus proved once and for all that we have a God who desires not to condemn us, but rather, to save us. We have a God who came so that we might not perish because of our sins and weakness, but rather, came so that we might receive eternal life.

We touch our head as we say the name "Father", remembering that God the Father is the Creator of all things. We remember that before we ever existed in this world, we existed in the mind of God the Father, our Creator, who has always loved us.

We then lower our hand as we focus on God the Son who came down from heaven and humbled himself, becoming flesh to reveal to us God's passionate love for us on the cross.

Then we cross our shoulders as we direct our attention to the Holy Spirit. As we touch our shoulders, we recall that the Holy Spirit is dwelling within us. We do not shoulder our burdens alone! God's Spirit is dwelling within us as our advocate, our helper in our daily lives.

The words we say making the Sign of the Cross are packed full of meaning. "In the name of the Father, and of the Son, and of the Holy Spirit". These words echo the celebration of Baptism when the Father, the Son, and the Holy Spirit welcomed us into their divine life. At our Baptism, we became God's adopted children. We received the Holy Spirit within our souls so that we can confidently call God, *Abba*, a loving parent, and call Jesus our brother.

Being able to address God *by name* is a big deal.

In the Old Testament, God's revelation of his name was something incredibly special for Moses and the people of Israel. God revealing his name to his people meant that God did not desire an anonymous relationship with them, but a personal relationship and intimate friendship with them.

The same is true for us.

At our Baptism, the minister said: "I baptize you in the *name* of the Father, and of the Son, and of the Holy Spirit." At this moment, God chose to associate us with his name. God chose to give us the ability to address him by name in a relationship of closeness and familiarity that no human person could ever earn on their own or be worthy to enjoy. At our Baptism, the three persons of the Trinity claimed us their own, as a member of God's family. When we sign ourselves in the name of the Father, the Son, and the Holy Spirit we remind ourselves who we belong to, who cares for us, and who loves us. The Sign of the Cross is an act of faith in our special relationship with God our loving Father, Jesus our Brother, and the Holy Spirit who dwells in our hearts.

The Sign of the Cross at the beginning of Mass is an expression of how near God is to us and how much God loves us. When we make the Sign of the Cross we open ourselves to the love of the Trinity that Jesus revealed to us by his sacrifice on the Cross. This unconditional love of God for us pervades all of the rituals of the Mass.

Pope Benedict XVI captures the essence of this ancient gesture: "The Sign of the Cross is a kind of synthesis of our faith, for it tells how much God loves us; it tells us that there is a love in this world that is stronger than death, stronger than our weaknesses and sins."[1]

THE GREETING OF THE ASSEMBLED PEOPLE

The Priest:
The Lord be with you.
Or
The grace of our Lord Jesus Christ,
and the love of God,
and the communion of the Holy Spirit
be with you all.
Or
Grace to you and peace from God our Father
and the Lord Jesus Christ.
The people:
And with your spirit.

"God never gives us more than we can handle."

Many well-intentioned Christians share this cliché with people who are going through difficult times. This phrase is meant to provide reassurance and comfort.

The problem is that this phrase never appears in the Bible.

In fact, Sacred Scripture is filled with one story after another of people who God asked to do more than they could handle. The Bible is packed full of narratives describing moments when God's plan stretched people beyond the capabilities of their own talents, virtues, and competencies.

The lives of important figures in salvation history teach us that God always gives us more than we can handle on our own. These heroic figures of faith show us that the decisive choice a person must make in life is whether or not they will welcome God's presence into their life and allow God to lead them beyond their own plans for the future.

Some of the first words the priest speaks to the congregation during the Mass point out the opportunity we have to welcome God's presence into our life, especially during the Mass.

Oftentimes, going through the day, we allow our minds to focus on our problems, our frustrations, our difficulties, and situations causing us stress. Our minds easily fixate on how tired we are, how annoyed we have become, and how challenging life is most days.

The words of the priest at the beginning of the Mass encourage us to focus on something else. Or better yet, on Someone else.

The priest greets the assembled people saying: "The Lord be with you", "The grace of our Lord Jesus Christ, the love of God, and the communion of the Holy Spirit be with you all", or "Grace to you and peace from God our Father and the Lord Jesus Christ".

These words are both a statement of fact and a petition. They express how close God is to us already, and they are a prayer that our hearts will be open to welcoming God's presence during the Mass. These words center our attention on God who leads us beyond ourselves into the adventure God has planned for our lives.

These phrases the priest speaks at the beginning of the Mass originate in the Bible. "The Lord be with you" is a traditional Jewish greeting in the Old Testament, found specifically in Ruth 2:4. This phrase served as a way to greet poor laborers working in the fields. This friendly greeting was also a sincere prayer that God would help these suffering people in their struggles, their fatigue, and their labors.

Christians recognize that God answered this prayer through the birth of Jesus as Emmanuel, which means "God is with us" (see Matthew 1:23). The Son of God chose to enter into the struggles of our human condition, so that we would know that we are not alone when we are going through problems and suffering. The Lord is with us!

Thus, at the beginning of the Mass these words are both a friendly greeting to acknowledge that the congregation is already in relationship with God and a prayer that the congregation will experience God's presence in the Mass.

The phrase "the grace of our Lord Jesus Christ, and the love of God, and the communion of the Holy Spirit be with you all" comes from St. Paul who used these words both as a greeting and as a prayer in his writings to the early Christian communities (2 Corinthians 13:13). Another similar greeting of St. Paul is also an option for the beginning of Mass: "Grace to you and peace from God our Father and the Lord Jesus Christ". This greeting is present in many of the letters attributed to St. Paul: 2 Corinthians 1:2; Romans 1:7; 1 Corinthians 1:3; Galatians 1:3; Ephesians 1:2; Philippians 1:2; 2 Thessalonians 1:2; Philemon 3.

Certainly, these words were extremely important in the early Church as St. Paul's repeated use demonstrates.

They reinforce the same message of the Old Testament greeting "the Lord be with you", while giving emphasis to bonds of communion that God was forming among the members of the early Christian communities. This emphasis on unity is significant because usually the reason St. Paul wrote to early Christian communities was precisely because they were experiencing conflict, division, misunderstanding, and tension of some kind. Thus, this greeting and prayer of St. Paul was meant to say: "I know your community is facing challenges right now, but you do not need to solve these problems with your own talents and strength alone. God is present and working in your midst! I am praying that God's grace will work powerfully right now to bring you closer together."

At the beginning of the Mass, the priest says these words as a greeting and as a prayer to reawaken in our hearts a recognition that God is working in our midst, especially as we face tensions in our own communities. The priest's words ask God to work within each of us to bring us closer together as a community during the Mass.

The Lord will be with us in several ways during the Mass - through the words of the Bible, through the Eucharist, through the ministry of the priest, and through the Christian people gathered in the seats around us.

The response of the people to the priest's initial greeting highlights the distinct role of the priest during the Mass. The congregation says: "And with your spirit". Again, the wording comes from St. Paul's writings where he sought to underline the presence of God's Spirit working within the Christian community (see, for example, Galatians 6:18; Philippians 4:23; Philemon 25). Over time, the use of these words in the Mass became a conventual way to accentuate how the Spirit of the risen Jesus works in a particular way through the ordained minister. In fact, the congregation speaks the phrase "And with your spirit" four times during the Mass when the Spirit of the risen Jesus will work through the minister in a unique way. These are the Penitential Act, the proclamation of the Gospel, the Eucharistic Prayer, and the final blessing/sending at the end of Mass.

Therefore, the dialogue "the Lord be with you...and with your spirit" signals to us that the Spirit of the risen Jesus will be working through the ordained minister in the prayers that this dialogue and response are introducing. This exchange is a way of saying to us: "Focus on what Jesus is going to do now through the minister!".

This dialogue is a very helpful cue to recall that Jesus is the true leader of the Mass. Whether or not our favorite priest is celebrating the Mass is not what is most important. What is most important is that the Spirit of the risen Jesus will work through the priest during Mass. The priest might be young and athletic, old and frail, bald and fat, or have a beard and long hair. None of this really matters for the effectiveness of what is about to take place.

The key actor during the Mass is Jesus Christ, who died for us on the cross and is risen from the dead, who will act through the priest during the Mass. The role of the priest is not to entertain the congregation. He is a physical instrument whose words and actions the risen Jesus uses to speak to us and to act in our lives through the ritual of the Mass, drawing us deeper into the life of the Trinity.

The dialogue between the priest and the people at the beginning of Mass demonstrates that Catholic worship is not entertainment. The purpose of Catholic worship is not primarily to make us feel good or to give us an adrenaline rush. We go to Mass for something different - to have a personal encounter with the risen Jesus.

Unlike watching an action movie, attending a rock concert, or cheering on our favorite team at a sporting event, what is happening at Mass is profoundly relational and profoundly *sacred*. The Mass is all about a relationship, the relationship between God and his people. At Mass this relationship is ritually engaged, as God speaks to us through the words of the Bible and enters into a close rapport with us in the Eucharist.

Here, we encounter God's power and love through sacred ritual. Marriage therapists talk about how successful marriages and families have rituals that facilitate closeness and communication. For example, a couple may have coffee together every Saturday morning, or a monthly date night, or go for a walk every Sunday. A family may eat special meals on birthdays and enjoy traditions on Christmas and Easter. The purpose of these rituals in the life of a family is for people to *be* together and to grow closer together as a family.

Catholic worship is very similar. Just as rituals of family life contain amazing and profound moments alongside the everyday and the mundane, so too with Catholic worship we find ourselves having experiences that are both subtle and repetitive, while also being awesome and inspiring. In both, a relationship is deepening and growing stronger. Our friendship with God is intensifying.

Catholic liturgy challenges us to be more than consumers of Sunday worship, but rather, active participants. Making the effort to stay engaged requires us to exert ourselves. Dialogue and responses between the priest and people invite us to put *ourselves* into worship. Through the ritual of the Mass, we open ourselves to God and offer all that we are to the loving God who created us and died for us. The chapters of this book will unpack what this means at a practical level, enabling you to put yourself into the Mass.

THE PENITENTIAL ACT

The Priest:
Brothers and sisters, let us acknowledge our sins,
and so prepare ourselves to celebrate the sacred
  mysteries.
All:
I confess to almighty God
and to you, my brothers and sisters,
that I have greatly sinned,
in my thoughts and in my words,
in what I have done and in what I have failed to do,
through my fault, through my fault,
through my most grievous fault;
therefore I ask the blessed Mary ever-Virgin,
all the Angels and Saints,
and you, my brothers and sisters,
to pray for me to the Lord our God.
The Priest:
May almighty God have mercy on us,
forgive us our sins,
and bring us to everlasting life.
The people:
Amen.
The Priest, Deacon, or another minister:
Lord, have mercy. **Or:** *Kyrie, eleison.*
The people:
Lord, have mercy. **Or:** *Kyrie, eleison.*
The Priest, Deacon, or another minister:
Christ, have mercy. **Or:** *Christe, eleison.*

The people:
Christ, have mercy. Or: Christe, eleison.
The Priest, Deacon, or another minister:
Lord, have mercy. Or: Kyrie, eleison.
The people:
Lord, have mercy. Or: Kyrie, eleison.
Or
The Priest:
Have mercy on us, O Lord.
The people:
For we have sinned against you.
The Priest:
Show us, O Lord, your mercy.
The people:
And grant us your salvation.
The Priest:
May almighty God have mercy on us,
forgive us our sins,
and bring us to everlasting life.
The people:
Amen.
The Priest, Deacon, or another minister:
Lord, have mercy. Or: Kyrie, eleison.
The people:
Lord, have mercy. Or: Kyrie, eleison.
The Priest, Deacon, or another minister:
Christ, have mercy. Or: Christe, eleison.
The people:
Christ, have mercy. Or: Christe, eleison.
The Priest, Deacon, or another minister:
Lord, have mercy. Or: Kyrie, eleison.
The people:
Lord, have mercy. Or: Kyrie, eleison.
Or

The Priest, Deacon, or another minister:
You were sent to heal the contrite of heart of heart:
Lord, have mercy. **Or:** *Kyrie, eleison.*
The people:
Lord, have mercy. **Or:** *Kyrie, eleison.*
The Priest, Deacon, or another minister:
You came to call sinners:
Christ, have mercy. **Or:** *Christe, eleison.*
The people:
Christ, have mercy. **Or:** *Christe, eleison.*
The Priest, Deacon, or another minister:
You are seated at the right hand of the Father to
    intercede for us:
Lord, have mercy. **Or:** *Kyrie, eleison.*
The people:
Lord, have mercy. **Or:** *Kyrie, eleison.*
The Priest:
May almighty God have mercy on us,
forgive us our sins,
and bring us to everlasting life.
The people:
Amen.

During college, I lived in Austria for a semester. I studied with 200 other students from the United States who for that semester embraced the attitude of "don't let schoolbooks get in the way of your education". Each Thursday after our last class ended, we grabbed our travel backpacks and hurried off to the train station to explore Europe for the weekend.

And explore Europe we did. Over the course of four months, I travelled to Prague, Salzburg, Vienna, Munich, Paris, Florence, Venice, Rome, Krakow, and many other European cities large and small.

What I quickly discovered during that semester was that you learn a lot about other people when you travel with them. You see them not only when they are happy and comfortable, but also when they are tired, grouchy, stressed, hungry, confused, annoyed, lost, and uncomfortable. Travel with someone long enough and you eventually see them at their best and worst. You get to know who they are in a very raw, honest sort of way. In fact, they will inevitably annoy you, offend you, hurt you, or frustrate you at some point along the way.

Friendships I formed during those travels were some of the strongest relationships of my entire college experience. They were genuine friendships based on who we truly were, flaws and imperfections included. Stress and strain of travel forced us to put aside the masks, facades, and cosmetic treatments we typically used to hide our blemishes, literally and figuratively. With weaknesses exposed, our friendships became honest and authentic. Since our flaws could not be hidden, we had many opportunities to experience our humanity in a way that was raw and beautiful, vulnerable and affirming, humbling and exhilarating. Those friendships gave me a taste of unconditional love.

At the beginning of Mass, we recall God's unconditional love. The Penitential Act gives us an opportunity to engage with God in an honest friendship. Even though God has seen us at our weakest, darkest, and most broken moments, God still desires to share a friendship with us. We have offended and hurt God, but at the beginning of Mass we acknowledge our sins and experience the undeserved, and yet unconditionally given, mercy and love of God the Father.

The Penitential Act is a time to think about our sins. We call to mind our recent sins at the beginning of the Mass not for the sake of feeling terrible about ourselves, but rather to prepare ourselves to experience God's unconditional love and healing mercy. We call to mind our sins to ask for God's help in overcoming the specific sins that we have been struggling with at this particular time in our life. We acknowledge our weakness and guilt at this point in the Mass, so we can enter into a more honest and intimate relationship with God who desires to give us peace and forgiveness.

The words we use to ask for God's mercy at Mass are those

the Bible records people using to ask Jesus for his help. Ten lepers asked Jesus for healing crying out: "Lord, have mercy!" (Luke 17:13). Several blind people cried out "Lord, have mercy!" to beg Jesus to heal them (Matthew 9:27, 20:30-31; Mark 10:47-48; Luke 18:38-39). A woman whose daughter was tormented by a demon and a man whose son was possessed both cried out "Lord, have mercy!" as they worried over the fate of their loved ones (Matthew 15:22, 17:15).

Jesus responded to their requests by providing healing and freeing them from evil.

We pray these same words "Lord, have mercy" (*Kyrie, eleison* in Greek) to acknowledge our need for God's help in our lives. We acknowledge that our bad habits are eating away at us like leprosy and isolating us from other people. We acknowledge that our selfishness is blinding us to the needs of other people. We acknowledge that many of our loved ones are far away from God, obsessed with the wrong priorities, and stuck in evil tendencies. We cry out "Lord, have mercy" to open our hearts to Jesus who brings healing and freedom from sin in our lives.

As the priest prays the healing words "May Almighty God have mercy on us, forgive us our sins, and bring us to everlasting life", our venial sins are forgiven and our friendship with God is renewed. The Penitential Act reassures us that God, who has known us in our worst and ugliest moments, still chooses to love us!

Along with the other elements of the Introductory Rites, the Penitential Act prepares us to encounter God in the Liturgy of the Word and the Liturgy of the Eucharist. The Introductory Rites challenge us to be more vulnerable and honest as we encounter God in the Mass. Obviously, the all-knowing God knows us better than we know ourselves, so the purpose of this vulnerability is not for us to inform God of something. God already knows our weaknesses and our faults. The issue is on our side of the relationship – we often overlook how much we need God's mercy.

The Penitential Act pushes us to be honest with ourselves

about our sinfulness. This helps us grasp how much we need to be cooperative and attentive to all that God offers us during the Mass. Our pride is a huge obstacle we place in front of the great work God can do for us during the Mass. The Introductory Rites detach us from the prideful masks of perfection we wear. They challenge us to let go of our stubborn attempts at self-sufficiency. They lead us to accept God's unconditional love for us as we truly are – broken, weak, and sinful.

In this way, the Penitential Act prepares us for the Gloria. We praise and adore the merciful God who pursues sinners, enters into the imperfect situations of their lives, and redeems them.

THE GLORIA IN EXCELSIS

Glory to God in the highest,
and on earth peace to people of good will.

We praise you,
we bless you,
we adore you,
we glorify you,
we give you thanks for your great glory,
Lord God, heavenly King,
O God, almighty Father.

Lord Jesus Christ, Only Begotten Son,
Lord God, Lamb of God, Son of the Father,
you take away the sins of the world,
    have mercy on us;
you take away the sins of the world,
    receive our prayer;
you are seated at the right hand of the Father,
    have mercy on us.

For you alone are the Holy One,
you alone are the Lord,
you alone are the Most High,
Jesus Christ,
with the Holy Spirit,
in the glory of God the Father.
Amen.

Sometimes what we see happening around us at the Mass can be less than edifying.

We notice an elderly person nodding off to sleep. Energetic toddlers throw small toys into the backs of people seated nearby. An altar server digs into his nose to clear a disgusting booger. A cantor cannot find the right note to lead others in song.

The Mass can be a very earthly experience sometimes. Sometimes, so distracting and messy that we wonder whether it is really worth our effort to attend.

When I think of disconcerting, messy, earthly experiences, my first trip to Bethlehem comes immediately to mind.

A seminarian at the time, I was very excited to visit the Holy Land. Learning that we would be visiting Bethlehem, my mind filled with romantic and beautiful ideas of what Bethlehem would be like. I thought of the peaceful Christmas manger scene I saw as a child at the local church every Christmas. I also recalled the less elaborate, but equally beautiful manger scene under our Christmas tree. And Christmas carols, which always made me feel good about the Christmas season, led me to imagine Bethlehem as a very charming city.

Yet, when our charter bus arrived, I was very disappointed by what I saw. In fact, before we could even enter into Bethlehem, our bus stopped at a wall. Not a picturesque ancient city wall, but instead a large and ugly cement wall with electrified barbed wire on top. Unsettling graffiti covered it. Before we could pass through, several armed soldiers entered our bus for elaborate border control protocols. This was my first lesson about the many years of ugly, violent conflict between the Palestinians and Israelis. Needless to say, it was not a sight that brought Christmas peace to my heart.

As we finally arrived in the city, the first place I wanted to visit was the Church of the Nativity, built over the very spot where Mary gave birth to Jesus. Approaching the square in front of the church, I heard shouting and gun-shots. The commotion was from people celebrating results of a local election by shooting guns into the air. The shooting and shouting did not bring much comfort and joy to the heart of someone who had grown up in a peaceful neighborhood in rural Ohio.

Entering the church from that loud and chaotic town square, Manger Square, I held my breath in anticipation of the great splendor of the holy place.

Once inside though, I was tremendously disappointed by what I saw. The very tired church building was less than spectacular. It was in obvious need of repair and a good cleaning. The sad reason why the church was so dirty was various Christian denominations who share the building were so hostile to each other that they could not cooperate on even a simple task as cleaning the church.

At the front of the church, a set of steps led downstairs to the place where Jesus was born. The guide book described how this small cave served as a stable for animals at the time of Jesus' birth. Descending into this chapel, I again couldn't help but think of the beautiful, romantic Christmas crib scenes from my childhood.

At the bottom of the steps, I stopped. Was I in the right place?

There was nothing overly attractive about this small area. It was dull, dismal, and dirty.

I was again disappointed.

Only a few other people were praying in the damp, dimly lit room that evening, so I knelt on the cold floor to spend some time in prayer. Looking up, I noticed the ceiling of this small cave was not covered in gold or silver, nor beautiful frescoes. Instead the ceiling was dirty, black from the soot of candles lit by pilgrims and it appeared that no one had cleaned the place in years. On the walls hung unimpressive paintings that looked like they too hadn't been cleaned or even dusted in decades.

As I knelt and tried to pray, I couldn't help but focus on my disappointment. Why had God chosen Bethlehem? Why enter our world in a place that was so unimpressive and imperfect? Why enter our world in a city that would be torn apart by war and violence for centuries? Why not the beautiful and charming city as I had imagined Bethlehem would be? Why did God choose a place unattractive, dirty, and poor?

Kneeling in that unimpressive space, the answer to my questions became very clear. This was precisely the whole point. The reason God chose the city of Bethlehem was precisely so that we would know that God desires to be near to us not just when our lives are beautiful, romantic, and perfect. God entered our world in the poor and unattractive city of Bethlehem, so that we would know that God desires to be near to us most especially when our lives are imperfect or a mess.

The gospel of John tells us that "the Word became flesh and made his dwelling among us" (John 1:14). The Son of God (the Word of God), became flesh and dwelt amongst us in the real world! The Son of God entered into human existence in a world filled with violence and war, in our world that can be so cruel and dirty, so disappointing and imperfect, filled with poverty and weakness, so very dark. In *our* world, "the Son of God became flesh and made his dwelling amongst us".

Praying that day in Bethlehem, it became clear that if God was willing to become present there, he is willing to become present anywhere. If God was willing to enter into the poverty of Bethlehem, he could enter into anyone's life no matter how weak, broken, or worthless they might feel.

The gospel of Luke recounts that when Jesus was born, angels appeared to humble shepherds surrounded by their smelly sheep outside Bethlehem and the angels sang: "Glory to God in the highest and on earth peace to those on whom his favor rests" (Luke 2:14).

During the Gloria at Mass, we join in this song of the angels at Bethlehem. We express praise and gratitude, as we celebrate God's choice to enter into our messy, dysfunctional, and disconcerting world. We sing praise to God for overcoming the power of sin and winning the ultimate victory over evil that creates so much chaos and disappointment in life. We rejoice that God's light is stronger than the darkness of our broken world.

The Gloria is a prayer of praise. At a natural human level,

praising others is something many of us do regularly. We stand up, clap, and raise our voices when our favorite quarterback throws a touchdown, or when our favorite musician finishes a performance, or when a colleague wins a big contract for our company. Gestures of praise express our excitement about someone and the good they have accomplished.

We sing the Gloria to acknowledge our excitement about who God is and how God's great power is at work here on earth. During the Gloria, we celebrate and praise God who does not distance himself from brokenness, but instead chose to make his dwelling in humble places like Bethlehem and our own lives. We praise God for the gift of the Incarnation, God's choice to enter into our midst to bring us salvation. Through the words of the Gloria, we praise God for being willing to come into our lives in powerful ways *today*, precisely through the celebration of the Mass.

THE COLLECT

The Catholic did not know how to respond.

A Catholic university student made an appointment with me to discuss his relationship with his new girlfriend. As it turned out, the reason for meeting was to pose several questions that his new girlfriend had asked after attending Mass for the first time. She had grown up in an Evangelical Christian church whose Sunday services were very different than the Catholic Mass. Her Catholic boyfriend did not know how to respond to most of her questions.

One major complaint she had about the Mass was that there was no place to offer personal prayers. She complained that the prayers of the Mass were too generic. She felt like a spectator watching the priest rattle on and on as he read impersonal prayers from a big book. She was annoyed that there was no time during the Mass when she could share her deepest needs with God.

I explained to her Catholic boyfriend that there are many places during the Mass when we are supposed to offer our personal prayers to God. Several places during the Mass, time is set aside for us to speak to God from the heart and bring our special intentions and needs to God.

After the Gloria, the priest says "Let us pray". Then there is usually a pause that can seem superfluous and awkward, as the priest seemingly waits for the altar server to bring the book over to him to read a prayer.

This pause is actually intentional.[2]

It is a time to call to mind intentions we would like to offer to God at Mass. This is a time to remember God desires to provide help, strength, guidance, support, and inspiration to his people. The intentions we offer during this silence might vary from week to week. One week we may be praying for God's help with our own health issues, financial worries, or relationship struggles. Another week we may be praying for a friend suffering from cancer, a neighbor going through a painful divorce, or a sibling dealing with depression. Some weeks our prayers may be for an end to war in a foreign country or for greater wisdom and civility among politicians in our own country.

The prayer the priest eventually reads after an intentional pause is called the "Collect", which comes from the Latin verb that means "to draw up, to collect". The Collect is meant to collect together all the prayers we each individually bring to the Mass. In fact, you will notice the Collect is usually somewhat generic. The prayer is not more specific for a reason. It is a general prayer that draws together all the prayers in our hearts and directs all of us to God who we encounter in the Liturgy of the Word.

During the Mass, there are several other moments when the words prayed by the priest seem broad and are intentionally not overly specific, precisely because they are meant to unite the personal prayers of all the people gathered at Mass and direct these prayers to Almighty God. Whenever there is a pause in the movement or the words of the Liturgy, there is an opportunity for us to enter into dialogue with God, as we share our deepest thoughts, feelings, and choices with God and listen quietly for a divine response.

The Collect concludes the Introductory Rites. The main purpose of this part of the Mass is preparation. Preparing us to enter as fully as possible into an encounter with the Trinity in the Liturgy of the Word and the Liturgy of the Eucharist. The

Introductory Rites stimulate our reflection on our life journey and draw us into deeper awareness that God wants to share our journey with us. The prayers that begin the Mass also lead us to recognize that we are not on this journey with God alone. We share it with the community of people who God has put into our lives and gathered at the Mass.

THE LITURGY OF
THE WORD

THE FIRST READING

I was afraid of the unknown.

At a certain point towards the end of college, I became very afraid and anxious about my future. I spent much time praying and thinking about my next step after graduation. I had asked mentors for their advice about my future and they said that going to seminary seemed to be a good fit for me.

However, I was still very uncomfortable with the idea of going to seminary.

Would I be miserable there? Would living celibacy make me become weird and a loner? Should I give up other exciting career options and a beautiful romantic relationship with the woman of my dreams?

During this tumultuous period of my life, I was attending Mass during one Sunday in Lent when the first reading from the Old Testament told a story from the life of Abram. At a certain point in Abram's life, God asked him to leave behind everything familiar and comfortable, to set off on a journey into the unknown. "The LORD said to Abram: "Go forth from the land of your kinsfolk and from your father's house to a land that I will show you"" (Genesis 12:1). God's request to Abram was especially demanding, considering how closely attached people were to their land in that culture.

Setting out on a journey with his large household would have been very stressful for Abram. Google maps did not yet exist. There was no guarantee they would find shelter or food along the way. This was millennia before Holiday Inns and fast food restaurants. Abram didn't know if other tribes along the way would see his family as a threat, attack, and try to kill them. Furthermore, the actual destination of the journey was open-ended. Abram did not know where God would lead him. All he knew was that God had asked him to begin a journey into the unknown and promised that he would take care of Abram and his family.

Despite all the reasons why Abram would have preferred not to make this journey, Genesis 12:4 tells us: "Abram went as the LORD directed him."

Listening to this reading at Mass, I felt a deep conviction in my heart that God was making the same request of me. Asking me to set out on a journey, even though I did not have all the answers about my future. Asking me to trust him and allow him to lead me beyond what was familiar and comfortable.

On that same Sunday, as Mass continued, the gospel reading was Matthew 17:1-9. Jesus' disciples were afraid and confused, so Jesus said to them: "Rise, and do not be afraid" (Matthew 17:7). When I heard those words, they were a reaffirmation of what God was saying to me in the first reading. The message was simple: "Get up and move forward to enter seminary. Don't be afraid!"

What I experienced during that Sunday Mass was the power of God's Word in the Bible. I understood what the Letter to the Hebrews affirms about God's ability to use the words of Sacred Scripture to speak to us: "Indeed, the word of God is living and effective, sharper than any two-edged sword, penetrating even between soul and spirit, joints and marrow, and able to discern reflections and thoughts of the heart." (Hebrews 4:12)

The words of the Bible have the potential to speak to us personally every single Sunday during the Liturgy of the Word at

Mass.

But why don't we experience the readings at Mass this way? Why don't we have a life-changing experience every time the readings are proclaimed?

One reason is the simple fact that Sunday Mass is a rare occasion during our week when typical sources of unrelenting stimuli are silent. We silence our cell phone. Close our tablet. Pause our playlist. Stop scrolling social media.

Fast-paced lifestyles have trained our minds to jump quickly between many sources of stimuli. Our minds do not stay focused easily. The relative calm of the Liturgy of the Word can quickly become a space to think about our to-do list and upcoming projects.

Thus, it is crucial when we sit down for the readings at Mass to decide to listen as attentively as possible. Reminding ourselves of God's ability to speak to us through the words of the Bible can help us approach the words of Sacred Scripture with reverence and attentiveness.

It can be very tempting to take for granted how easily we can access the Bible in our modern world. Around 1439 Johannes Gutenberg pioneered the use of movable print type and the printing press in Europe, which made it possible for Christians to have more access to the Bible outside of the Mass.

Before 1439 the Bible had its natural home in the Mass. In fact, thanks to the Catholic Mass we have the Bible as we know it today. The Mass was the primary and often the only place where people heard Sacred Scripture. In those days Christians did not have a Bible at home to read, study, and pray with on their own. Even the clergy and preachers did not always have personal access to the Old Testament or the New Testament in their residences. They simply had to remember what they heard when a section of the Bible was proclaimed during the Liturgy. The fact that many important teachers in the early Church, the Church Fathers, quoted various books of the Bible so frequently and so accurately demonstrates how they approached opportunities to hear the Bible as precious moments deserving their full focus and attention.

Whether we realize it or not, each Sunday we have an important choice to make. We can choose to allow God to speak to us or we can choose not to give God our full attention.

It is fascinating to watch passengers on an airplane during the safety demonstration at the beginning of a flight. People are usually quiet and respectful, but in reality, they are not paying attention to the video or the crew. One or two passengers might raise their heads from a book or take off their headphones to listen, but for the most part, the majority completely ignores the safety presentation. Very few, if any, follow the instructions to review the safety card in the seat pocket in front of them or look around to locate the nearest exit. Frequent flyers have heard the same words so many times that they believe giving their full attention is not worth the effort.

This same attitude, unfortunately, can become our default approach at Mass as well. Many of us have heard the same Bible stories at Mass from the time we were little children. It can be easy to sit in the pew and be "listening", but not *really* listening as Scripture passages are repeated.

However, the words of the Bible contain incredible power even if we have already heard them before. The Holy Spirit inspired the authors of the texts and that same Spirit uses these texts today to speak to our hearts, our needs, our problems, our decisions, and our experiences - if we are attentively listening.

Ask yourself during the readings at Mass: What is God saying to me today through these readings?

Listen carefully and God will speak to you.

Many times during the readings and the homily, it has been very clear to me that a certain theme was God's message to me for that week. Something spoke to what I was going through at that time. The words put my problems in context. They gave me direction on how to make better decisions. They offered insight into God's love for me and my true identity.

Other times at Mass, I have made a conscious decision to listen attentively to the readings and nothing happened. Nothing seemed to speak to me. Nothing clearly struck me as being relevant to my life in that moment.

What I've learned is that patience is necessary to receive God's message. Sometimes God will use what we hear at Mass to speak to us later in the week or some other time in the future. It might be several days after a Sunday Mass when we face a particular challenge at work when the readings will speak to us and become relevant to our lives. Or it might be Monday evening when we are in the middle of a conversation with a friend when a particular theme from the readings suddenly applies to our life situation in way that we had not thought of during Mass.

Some books of the Bible are more difficult to understand than others. Some days our ability to focus is greater than others. We will have our favorite readings and our favorite preachers. However, in all these situations we believe that "in the sacred books, the Father who is in heaven meets His children with great love and speaks with them".[3]

Roman Catholic communities throughout the world read the same Scripture readings on Sundays. They are contained in a book called the Lectionary and follow a three-year cycle. During Year A, the gospel reading is usually from the gospel of Matthew. During Year B, it is from the gospel of Mark and chapter 6 of the gospel of John. During Year C, it is from the gospel of Luke. The Easter Season in all years (A, B, C) features selections from the gospel of John.

The Roman Catholic Church throughout the world also reads specific readings during weekday Masses. The first reading and the Psalm are on a two-year cycle, while the gospel selections repeat annually.

All in all, during weekdays and weekends, the Catholic Church reads a combined total of over 70% of the New Testament and over 13% of the Old Testament in the lectionary.[4]

During the season of Ordinary Time, the first reading at Sunday Mass is from the Old Testament, which is the collection of books written before Jesus' birth. The first reading is not a random selection, but has been chosen to connect with the gospel reading. Since there is an intended common theme between these two, we can ask ourselves as we listen to the first reading and the gospel: What do these two readings have in common?

Determining the answer not only can keep us engaged during the readings, but also will lead us to see how the Old Testament prepared for the definitive revelation of God in the person of Jesus Christ in the New Testament.

That is what happened when I was listening to the readings on that Sunday in Lent back in college. God used a common theme from the first reading and the gospel to encourage me not to be afraid and to set out on the journey God had prepared for my future.

It is a great privilege to have a relationship with the God of the universe who desires to speak with us. At the end of the first reading and the second reading the lector says: "The Word of the Lord" pointing out that God just spoke to us through the humble, human words of the Bible. The assembly responds: "Thanks be to God". Gratitude is the proper response to a God who speaks to our hearts through the readings, shares divine insight with us, puts our earthly problems in perspective, and assures us that we are loved for all eternity.

THE RESPONSORIAL PSALM

"What? Are you serious?", the student asked me with a tone of acute skepticism and continued: "I am sure we are not supposed to talk to God like that."

I gently repeated what I had just said to her: "It is OK to tell God how angry you are right now."

The young woman had been crying for several minutes before this point in our conversation and she squinted through moist eyelids with a pained expression on her face, not believing what I was saying. She was grieving deeply because her sister had just died unexpectedly. This tragic death made no sense to her. It seemed so unfair. And much of her deep anger was directed at God. She said it felt like God had abandoned her.

Searching for a way to explain to the grieving woman, a graduate student, that she could be honest with God about her feelings, I encouraged her to read some Psalms from the Old Testament.

I suggested Psalm 22 which begins with the words:

My God, my God, why have you abandoned me?
Why are you so far from my call for help,
from my cries of anguish?
My God, I call by day, but you do not answer;
by night, but I have no relief.

Several other Psalms express similarly strong feelings of anger, sadness, and frustration, and I encouraged her to pray them during the upcoming weeks. I told her not to be afraid to put her emotions into these strong words from the Scriptures because Jesus himself prayed these words many times during his life, according to the typical Jewish custom. In fact, Jesus prayed Psalm 22 as he was dying on the cross (Matthew 27:46; Mark 15:34).

About a month later, the student returned to tell me that praying the Psalms as she grieved had been life-changing for her. The Psalms had helped her express her deepest human emotions, while leading her to put her trust in God.

During the Mass, a Psalm from the Old Testament is read or sung after the first reading. It can often be the "forgotten reading", considered wrongly as a musical break between readings. Overlooking the Psalms is a tragic mistake because they are rich with meaning and extremely relevant to our lives.

The Psalms are 150 different prayers from the Old Testament that poetically express a full-range of human emotions and experiences. In some, the speaker expresses uncontainable joy in a time of celebration, elation, and excitement. Other moments, the speaker cries out to God in fright, anger, sadness, or disappointment. Other Psalms express desires associated with more mundane realities of work and family life.

The candid language of the Psalms should lead us to speak honestly to God about what is going on in our lives. Those of us who hesitate during Mass to share with God our human feelings, thoughts, and questions because they are too raw or too negative should remember that the Son of God, Jesus Christ, prayed the full range of human expressions contained in the Psalms. In fact, even the darker Psalms like Psalm 22 have threads of trust and hope woven through them. The Psalms help the one praying to accept that God is present in *all* situations of life, even where God seems distant or absent.

This honesty about reality is why the Psalms are such a great gift. Every Psalm helps us to be honest with God, but also entrust our future and our life into God's hands even when the divine plan does not make sense to us.

Sometimes making our own the words of the Psalm during the Mass is very easy. During a fun weekend, words from a joyful and upbeat Psalm will pair well with our situation. After a challenging week, we will relate easily to a Psalm that expresses deep sadness, confusion, or pain.

In other moments, when the Psalm does not match our own experience, it is helpful to enter into it as an act of solidarity with people who can relate to its theme because of what they are going through right now. For example, if the Psalm is focused on joy and gratitude, we can pray the words of that Psalm in prayerful solidarity and intercession for a friend or coworker who is going through an exciting time in their life. If the Psalm is focused on sadness and pain, we can pray those words in prayerful solidarity and intercession for a family member or colleague battling a serious illness, going through a divorce, or struggling financially. Praying the Psalms in this way brings us closer together as a faith community who shares the joys and sorrows of life together.

Ultimately, praying the Psalms is a great privilege because we are uniting our voices to the voice of the Son of God, Jesus Christ. Through the Psalms, Jesus guides our prayer and teaches us to speak honestly to God the Father. We are supposed to speak to God like that!

THE SECOND READING

There was a difference of only one letter between his two names.

He was very intelligent and well-educated. From a respectable family and well-connected. Passionate about his beliefs, especially his religious convictions, he had no patience for anyone who saw things differently than he did. Quick to judge other people, he was also quick to anger and lose his patience. He spoke out boldly, strongly, and passionately condemned those who did not see the world as he did.

While he would never have admitted it at the time, he was actually deeply insecure inside and felt threatened by those who held different beliefs. His impulsive nature, deep anger, fear, and impatience led him to harass people whose beliefs disturbed him.

Then he started killing them.

This man was Saul of Tarsus.

And yet, something happened in his life that changed Saul of Tarsus. In fact, so much changed inside Saul of Tarsus that people felt the need to call him by a different name: Paul.

Paul was certainly still passionate and intense. Still deeply convicted and bold in his lifestyle and beliefs. And yet, very different than the impulsive, impatient, and hateful man everyone called Saul of Tarsus.

Suddenly, Paul was patient, merciful, and generous. Encouraging, loving, and no longer hatefully condemning. He was living the challenging and demanding teachings of Jesus.

The difference (in English) between the names Saul and Paul is only one letter, but the difference between the two lifestyles these names represent is tremendous.

A sinful way of life led Saul of Tarsus to be known by all as a murderer.

Encountering Jesus Christ changed Saul of Tarsus into the man who people called Paul, one of the greatest Christian apostles who has ever lived. St. Paul was able to go beyond his pride, his insecurity, his condemning and hateful ways because of the power of Jesus working in his soul.

The same is true for us! The writings of St. Paul teach us that Jesus' power makes it possible for us to be transformed from Saul into Paul. This great apostle's writings teach us how to be transformed from sinners into saints. His letters share with us the wisdom he gained from his personal experience of going through a life-changing transformation.

Usually the second reading during Sunday Mass comes from St. Paul's writings. Occasionally it will come from another New Testament author, but most Sundays we hear from a letter attributed to St. Paul. It should be noted that the second reading during a Sunday Mass is not necessarily selected to match the first reading, the Psalm, or the gospel during Ordinary Time. The second readings are designed to lead us week-by-week through a systematic reading of the New Testament letters, which means we usually hear highlights from the same letter for several consecutive Sundays.

For special seasons like Advent, Christmas, Lent, Easter, or special feast days, the Church has selected all of the readings (first reading, Psalm, second reading, and gospel) particularly for the day so they all share a common theme.

Reading New Testament letters during Sunday Mass has its roots in the early days of Christianity. During Sunday gatherings in the first century, Christians read from the letters that the apostles had written to their communities. The Church eventually compiled these letters into what we refer to as the New Testament.

Early Christians handed on these writings to future generations because these messages had changed their lives. The words of apostles like St. Paul contained life-changing truths that led early Christians into an intimate friendship with Jesus and helped them faithfully live an authentic Christian lifestyle.

There are common themes in St. Paul's letters. Looking for them during the second reading can help you perceive what God is saying, even when the language of a particular selection might be difficult to understand.

One major theme for St. Paul is God's mercy. St. Paul recognized he had made mistakes in the past. He understood that he did not deserve to be an important leader in the Church. The only explanation for why God had chosen him is that God gives second-chances. God does not abandon us when we make mistakes. God's mercy is transformative, not just pardoning past sins, but rehabilitating us, restoring what sin has damaged, and raising us up to fulfill a higher calling. God will often use the words of St. Paul to remind us that we are not beyond repair, we are capable of overcoming struggles with sin that discourage us.

A related theme is humility. St. Paul's arrogance as a young man led to many mistakes. He had taken great pride in his religious activism. He spent much time in self-congratulatory behavior, overlooking his own faults, and growing in his condescending criticism of others. His main focus was what *he* was doing. He forgot that God's work and grace were more important than his own efforts. He neglected to keep in mind that God is the only one who can give us salvation. For this reason, St. Paul's letters warn against trusting in human efforts alone and forgetting about God's grace. When we make our own good deeds and spiritual perfection into idols, even when our intention is to serve God, we can become controlling, selfish, and even vicious. The second reading often challenges us to let go of perfectionistic attempts to control everything, trusting instead in God's grace working in the complex relationships and situations of our lives.

Another deep conviction for St. Paul was the importance of seeking truth. Many of St. Paul's letters addressed Christianity communities where the truth was being distorted by trendy teachers. What God revealed mattered to St. Paul. Christianity was not a democratic supermarket of ideas where Christians pick and choose which teachings of Jesus they follow or leave behind. St. Paul travelled many miles and wrote many impassioned letters to plead with Christians to stay true to the teaching he had taught them, not allowing more popularized versions of Christianity to lead them astray. The numerous insults, beatings, and imprisonments St. Paul endured demonstrated to early Christians that he had staked his life on the truth. This witness helped inspire Christians to avoid popular immoral behaviors, taking the risk to live differently according to the truth Christ had revealed. When we are tempted to cave into peer pressure and avoid counter-cultural choices, Pauline teachings in the second reading encourage us to follow the truth Jesus taught.

A common thread in St. Paul's letters is the significance of Christian community. Frequently, St. Paul addressed disagreements, personality conflicts, and other drama within Christian communities. Despite these headaches, St. Paul constantly reminded Christians that sharing life with other people is essential to the Christian life. St. Paul insisted that being a member of the Body of Christ - the Christian community, includes responsibilities that cannot be shed when there is tension in a community. Christ and his Body are inseparable, so we cannot separate ourselves from the Body without distancing ourselves from Christ, the Head of the Church. St. Paul's letters contain a healthy dose of realism about challenges and frustrations of being involved in a faith community, but also provide needed encouragement not to walk away from these relationships when there is turmoil in our parish.

The singular, uniting focus of St. Paul's writings is the person of Jesus Christ. St. Paul did not consider Jesus to be just a famous wisdom figure, spiritual guru, or moral teacher. He was the Son of God who entered into the human condition, suffered and died on the cross, rose from the dead, and is alive today, acting in history through the Church. There was nothing more real or important to St. Paul than his relationship with Jesus. St. Paul desired to introduce Jesus to everyone, especially Gentiles, people who had not known God as revealed in the Scriptures. St. Paul shared with everyone that Jesus was not aloof from humanity after his resurrection, but could be encountered in the Church. The Pauline writings contain the most ancient account of the Last Supper and the institution of the Eucharist (1 Corinthians 11:23-26), demonstrating how central the Mass was to St. Paul's understanding of the Christian life.

In the end, the difference between Saul and Paul is a difference of one letter. However, the chasm between the two lifestyles these two names represent is vast and wide. St. Paul's letters are a guide book that leads us through the same process of transformation. Every Sunday through the second reading, we can learn how to choose the lifestyle of Paul rather than Saul. How to choose love rather than selfishness. How to be a sinner who Jesus makes into a saint.

THE ACCLAMATION BEFORE THE GOSPEL

Alleluia, alleluia.

The Priest:
Cleanse my heart and my lips, almighty God,
that I may worthily proclaim your holy Gospel.

"The one who sings, prays twice!"

That was the message I learned as a small child attending Catholic elementary school.

I can't say I ever knew for sure what "prays twice" was actually supposed to mean. I assumed that "praying twice" was a concept similar to "buy one get one free" donut day at the bakery or the coupon my parents would occasionally use to order two greasy pizzas on evenings when they did not feel like cooking dinner. For some reason, you received double points from God for singing rather than just saying your prayers. I assumed God must really like hearing us sing.

This idea of "the one who sings, prays twice" is often attributed to St. Augustine who in his teaching on the Psalms emphasized the great value of singing in Christian spirituality.[5] St. Augustine taught that the singing of sacred hymns can engage us at a deeper level than when we recite prayers without singing. Sacred hymns can lead us to praise God enthusiastically in ways that go beyond the power of spoken words.

Think, for example, about the power of music outside of a church setting.

Athletes listen to music in preparation for competitions and during workouts because upbeat music expresses their desire to succeed, fuels motivation, and assists concentration and focus.

Lovers listen to music that engages their feelings, maintains a romantic mood, and expresses their choice to celebrate their friendship in special moments, such as, a dance at a wedding reception.

Angry teenagers listen to loud music and harsh lyrics that echo their interior angst and feelings of frustration, loneliness, and anxiety. Their music reinforces their anger and conveys their choice to allow these sentiments color their attitude.

Simply put, music has the power to touch us and engage us at a very deep place within our souls. Music also has the potency to express deep emotions, feelings, attitudes, and choices.

In this way, music has great power in the spiritual life. Music during the Mass is not for entertainment, but to lead us to more intense prayer and an opening up of our entire person to a deep encounter with God. Hymns during the Mass assist us in our choice to praise God and to show our love for God who is present during the Mass.

Before the gospel reading, the assembly stands to sing the Alleluia. "Alleluia" is a Hebrew word that means "praise God".[6] The Old Testament Psalms use it to joyfully express gratitude and praise to God for his saving help. (for example, Psalms 111-113; Psalms 116-117; Psalms 146-150).

At Mass, we sing Alleluia to praise God who is present in our midst. We sing the Alleluia in gratitude for Jesus' presence and the saving help he gives us through the words of the gospel that the deacon or priest will proclaim. The Catholic Church teaches that God makes himself present through the words of the Bible as they are proclaimed at Mass. The Scripture readings at Mass are more than a book study, bible study, or academic analysis of ancient literature. God speaks to each of us personally through the words of the Sacred Text at Mass. The Alleluia expresses our joy at being able to have a personal encounter with Jesus during the proclamation of the Gospel.

The congregation stands during the Alleluia, as a sign of respect similar to how in the culture of the United States people stand when a judge, the President, or another dignitary enters a room. We stand as a sign of respect for God's presence in the proclamation of the Gospel.

In the early Church, the word Alleluia was particularly associated with the resurrection of Jesus from the dead. We sing the Alleluia during Mass because we believe the same living Jesus who was present to his disciples after his resurrection is also present in our midst during the proclamation of the Gospel. With the power of music, the Alleluia focuses our attention on Jesus who is with us to teach us and to speak loving words to us. An intense prayer, the Alleluia opens our spirit, mind, and body– our whole person including our emotions, to a life-changing encounter with God in the reading of the Gospel.

To further accentuate the sacredness of the encounter that takes place in the reading of the Gospel, oftentimes during the Alleluia there is a procession with the Book of the Gospels. It may include candles and incense. These symbols sharpen our focus on encountering the divine in the proclamation of the Gospel. As the priest moves to the place where he will read the gospel, which is called the ambo, he bows before the altar and prays: "Cleanse my heart and my lips, Almighty God, that I might worthily proclaim your holy Gospel". This prayer of purification points to the sacredness of the words that God speaks to the congregation through the voice of the priest or deacon.

Furthermore, the Alleluia and other moments of singing during the Mass echo the singing of the joyful celebration in heaven. The Book of Revelation uses singing as a way to describe the eternal life of celebration that is our Christian destiny in heaven (see, for example, Revelation 5:9-10; 14:2-3). We sing now during the Mass as a way of expressing our desire to one day be fully incorporated into the rhythm of celebration that is the Kingdom of Heaven.

THE GOSPEL

"Tell me who your friends are and I will tell you who you are."

A mentor used to repeat those words to me when I was in high school.

He was right. Our friends have a deep influence upon us. Their lifestyles rub off on us. We absorb their habits, their ways of saying certain things, their attitudes, and their sense of humor. Their way of viewing the world becomes part of our worldview. Their choices influence our choices.

Those we choose to spend time with and choose to listen to have a deep impact on our character and actions.

The reading of the gospel at Mass should be one of our most special encounters with a friend. The Lord Jesus Christ called us his friends and loves us more than any other friend on this earth (see John 15:15). Spending time with Jesus as a friend and listening to him speak to us through the words of the Gospel will lead us to become more like him.

Yet, Jesus is also more than a friend. He is the Son of God, which means that not only does his personality, worldview, attitudes, and lifestyle rub off on us when we spend time with him and listen to him, but also his divine power is released in our lives.

When the deacon or priest reading the Gospel announces "a reading from the holy Gospel according to...", we acknowledge God's presence in our midst during this sacred moment by responding: "Glory to you, O Lord". These words are accompanied by a profound gesture that is done so routinely each Sunday that we usually perform it mindlessly unless we have made a deliberate effort to remember its meaning.

Tracing a small cross with our thumb on our forehead signifies the prayer that God's word will have a place in our mind and thoughts. Tracing a small cross on our lips signifies the prayer that God's word will have a place in our words. Tracing a small cross on our chest signifies the prayer that God's word will have a place in our heart and our decisions.

How often do we allow God's word to influence us in these three areas?

Consider, what makes up the bulk of the thoughts you entertain in your mind each day? How many are good?

Sadly, many of us allow a long list of negative messages to pervade our thoughts as we go about daily life. Many of us need to change that "playlist" of negativity and replace it with the good news of God's love for us.

How often is our thinking dominated by thoughts rooted in our lack of self-worth or lack of self-esteem? Are we replaying over and over again the hurtful things people have said to us? Do we dwell excessively on thoughts of past mistakes, failures, and regrets?

During the Liturgy of the Word, we ask God to give us a new

way of thinking. To help us focus our minds on the greatness of his mercy, unconditional love for us, and hope-filled plan for our future. We trace the cross on our foreheads, praying that the mercy, unconditional love, and hope that Jesus gave us on the cross will permeate all of our thinking and imagining. We pray for God's wisdom, truth, and peace to guide our thinking.

At this point in the Mass, we also pray for a change in the way we speak.

The average person speaks thousands of words each day. One group of researchers concluded that the average person speaks between 15,000 and 16,000 words per day.[7]

Have you considered how you use the thousands of words you speak each day? How many have the sound of the Good News of Jesus in them? How many do not, but instead convey negativity, bitterness, envy, or cynicism?

We trace a small cross on our lips before the proclamation of the Gospel as a prayer asking Jesus to transform our ability to speak so that the words that come from our mouths express the love, truth, and hope Jesus' words bring to humanity.

We also trace a small cross on our chest as a prayer asking God's word to permeate the depths of our heart. In the Biblical world a person's "heart" is the deepest core of their being, the inner place where a person makes decisions. Thus, in asking God's word to find a place in our hearts, we are praying for Jesus' teaching to influence our decision making and choices.

Have you ever thought about all the other influences that dominate your heart on a regular basis?

For many of us, worries and fears have a controlling influence on our hearts.

We fear the future. We fear not being good enough. We fear failure. We worry about our health and the health of loved ones. We worry about our finances and reputation. We worry what other people will say. We fear having to endure pain and suffering.

Oftentimes, these worries and fears negatively skew our ability to make good decisions.

By making a small cross on our chest at this point in the Mass, we are asking the words of Good News proclaimed during the Gospel to cast unhealthy fear and worry from our hearts, so that we can make decisions based on the confidence that comes from our identity as God's beloved sons and daughters. The Liturgy of the Word puts our decision-making into perspective - God's perspective. Assuring us that God will guide us into the future.

At the conclusion of the proclamation of the Gospel, the priest or deacon says the words: "The Gospel of the Lord". "Gospel" is a Greek word that means "good news". The words of the Bible are ultimately a message of God's relentless love for humanity and a proclamation of God's ultimate victory over darkness. Our grateful response to this "Good News" is to say: "Praise to you, Lord Jesus Christ".

Then the deacon or priest quietly prays: "Through the words of the Gospel may our sins be wiped away". This prayer asks that Jesus' core message of divine mercy might be realized in us at the Mass. That what God has spoken through the human voice of the minister will changes the lives of the people who have listened to them and help them experience eternal salvation.

The next gesture of the deacon or priest is quite strange from a human perspective. The minister kisses the Book of the Gospels!

When was the last time you kissed a book?

Similar to the reverencing of the altar with a kiss at the beginning of the Mass, the kissing of the Book of the Gospels is a vivid reminder of the personal nature of what occurs during the proclamation of God's Word during Mass. God reaches out to his people and communicates with them.

The Bible is ultimately a love story - a story of God's love for humanity. The minister's reverent kiss of the book shows that this love story continues today. It points to the preciousness of God's revelation given to us through the words of the Bible. For several centuries, the custom was for all the people at Mass to kiss the Book of the Gospels during Mass to show their reverence for God's presence in the Liturgy of the Word and their recognition of the deep intimacy they were experiencing with God in that moment.

During the Liturgy of the Word, we encounter the *living* God. God the Father speaks his Word, his Truth, to us through the words of the Gospel proclaimed by the minister. The Holy Spirit works, using the voice of the minister, to inspire us. Our response to God's Word is not just an intellectual assent, but a choice to enter into friendship with the Word made flesh - Jesus. The more time and attention we give to this friendship, the greater impact it will have on our lives. The more Jesus will transform us into his likeness.

THE HOMILY

It was the worst homily ever.

The elderly, white-haired deacon was preaching on Sunday at a small-town parish where I was serving as a seminarian. His homilies were notoriously dry and boring. He leaned heavily on the carved oak ambo as he preached, reading slowly from several pages of notes in a monotone voice that could put even the most hyper of persons into deep REM sleep.

This particular Sunday his sermon was especially slow and painful. At a certain point, he dropped all of his notes onto the floor. The overweight deacon stopped his preaching and slowly reached down to pick up his papers. When he finally resumed preaching, my heart sunk as I realized what was happening. The old man had lost his place in the text! The deacon was preaching page two of his sermon for a second time. It felt like the longest homily ever.

I left Mass very frustrated that weekend. Mad because I had gotten nothing out of the homily even though I had tried to pay attention, it felt like a complete waste of my time.

A few days later, I faced a rather challenging situation. I was shocked when the deacon's homily was the first thing that came to mind. His message about forgiveness had described in almost perfect detail the situation I was facing. Even worse, page two of the homily that he repeated spoke directly to what I was dealing with that day.

I learned on that Wednesday how God can use dry, boring preachers to speak to our lives during the Mass.

The wise and eloquent preacher St. John Vianney once put it this way to his congregation:

My children, you listen when you like the preacher; but

*if the preacher does not suit you, you turn him into
ridicule. . .We must not think so much about the man.
It is not the body that we must attend to. Whatever the
priest may be, he is still the instrument that the good
God makes use of to distribute His holy Word. You pour
liquor through a funnel; whether it be made of gold or of
copper, if the liquor is good it will still be good.*[8]

While all of us might have favorite preachers (and least favorite preachers), God can speak to us through any ordained priest
or deacon preaching during the Mass regardless of their talent as
a public speaker. The purpose of the homily is not to entertain
us, but rather to help us reflect on the divinely inspired words of
the Bible through which God speaks to us. Interestingly enough,
even in the early days of Christianity St. Paul warned the Christian community against the danger of becoming too attached to
flashy preachers who excelled in their oratorical skills, but were
not authentically preaching the truth (see 2 Corinthians 11:4-6).

So what are we to do when the preacher is boring and less than
engaging?

One method to stay engaged during a boring homily is to
continue reflecting on the question: What is God saying to me
today? This can focus our attention on God and help us avoid the
temptation of spending the entire homily making a mental list
of the preacher's defects.

Another helpful tactic is to spend time before Mass looking
at the readings of the day. Being familiar with the readings of
the day will aid our efforts to follow a homily that is not as well
organized as we would prefer. Also useful is reading a reflection
or listening to a podcast on the Sunday readings before we go to
church. Insights from these resources can focus our meditation
as we try to stay engaged during a lackluster homily.

Take consolation in remembering that the Church has sur-
vived for 2,000 years not on the skill of preachers themselves,
but rather, on God's ability to use weak, humble instruments to
share his divine message with the world. The first band of apostles included fishermen and several other relatively uneducated

men whose preaching converted thousands not because of eloquence, but because the Holy Spirit was working through their voices. Say a prayer to the Holy Spirit during the Liturgy of the Word asking the Holy Spirit to inspire the preaching of the priest or deacon. It is also a good practice to pray that we will be open to hearing God through the humble minister in front of us.

After all, what seems to be the worst homily ever might just turn out to be what God uses to speak to our lives this week.

THE PROFESSION OF FAITH

I believe in one God,
the Father almighty,
maker of heaven and earth,
of all things visible and invisible.

I believe in one Lord Jesus Christ,
the Only Begotten Son of God,
born of the Father before all ages.
God from God, Light from Light,
true God from true God,
begotten, not made, consubstantial with the Father;
through him all things were made.
For us men and for our salvation
he came down from heaven,
and by the Holy Spirit was incarnate of the Virgin Mary,
and became man.

For our sake he was crucified under Pontius Pilate,
he suffered death and was buried,
and rose again on the third day
in accordance with the Scriptures.
He ascended into heaven
and is seated at the right hand of the Father.
He will come again in glory
to judge the living and the dead
and his kingdom will have no end.

I believe in the Holy Spirit, the Lord, the giver of life,

who proceeds from the Father and the Son,
who with the Father and the Son is adored and glorified,
who has spoken through the prophets.

I believe in one, holy, catholic and apostolic Church.
I confess one Baptism for the forgiveness of sins
and I look forward to the resurrection of the dead
and the life of the world to come. Amen.

The Apostles Creed may be used instead of the Nicene Creed.

I was enjoying my mixed greens salad during lunch at a restaurant, when a friend asked me a provocative question. Starting sheepishly, suddenly he went right for it. "I know you are a priest, but do you ever find yourself wondering whether it is all actually true? Have you ever wondered whether what we as Christians believe about God is all really true?"

From the first days of the early Church, countless people have asked the same questions. We should not be embarrassed if we have pondered these questions ourselves. After all, Jesus' closest apostles experienced many doubts before arriving at a point of clarity in their own faith.

For example, the apostles felt fear, terror, and despair because of what took place on Good Friday. On that day the darkness and cruelty of the crucifixion, Jesus' seeming utter powerlessness, and the reality of his dead corpse buried in a tomb led the apostles to the conclusion that it was all really *not* true. It seemed they had been misled. The events of Good Friday seemed to prove that Jesus really was not God and their past experiences of his divine wisdom and power were illusions.

A complete transformation took place a few days later in this group of sad, despairing, and disenchanted apostles.

Something happened in the days after Good Friday that transformed their disbelief into a belief so passionate that they would stake their lives on the claim that Jesus was, in fact, the Son of God. These apostles would eventually endure tremendous torture and painful martyrdoms because of this belief. If the story of the resurrection had been made up, at some point in the torture of their painful martyrdoms they would have admitted it was all a lie.

A simple renunciation of their belief in Jesus' resurrection would have freed them, saving them from martyrdom.

Not one of these apostles gave up their profession of faith.

What they had seen and heard after Jesus' resurrection was too powerful to deny. It was all true! Jesus really was God! They had experienced Jesus risen from the dead and were utterly convinced of his divinity.

The apostles' faith was further bolstered by the Holy Spirit's action in their lives after Jesus ascended into heaven. The Holy Spirit had given them strength to proclaim boldly and persuasively the truths that Jesus had taught them. The Holy Spirit led them to teach and preach these truths in ways that went way beyond their own talents and natural abilities.

Now for centuries, the Catholic Church has handed on these truths throughout the entire world. In fact, perhaps the greatest proof that the Jesus is alive, risen from the dead, and still active in the world is that the Catholic Church continues to stand today and teach the truth despite many scandals and mistakes of its leaders and members over the centuries.

Every time we profess the Creed at Mass on Sunday, we are uniting our voices with the millions from past and present who entertained doubts, asked hard questions, and concluded that what the apostles taught is true. Yes, what the Catholic Church teaches really is true.

It is important to recognize what this choice to believe cost many early Christians. Their choice meant tremendous personal risk, especially in the Roman Empire where they faced persecution for most of the first three hundred years Christianity existed.

Professing the Creed at Mass on Sunday, we unite our voices with the profession of faith made by the apostles as they travelled throughout the world preaching about Jesus.

When we profess the words of the Creed at Mass, we show our agreement with theological propositions that we are reciting, while also entrusting our life to the God who we just encountered in the Liturgy of the Word.

Throughout the Creed as we state "I believe", we are saying "I give my heart and entrust my life to God the Father, to God the Son, and to God the Holy Spirit who are present and active in the one, holy, catholic, and apostolic Church today."

Praying the Creed is a time during the Mass when we consciously choose to entrust our future to God's care.

A few years ago, researchers from Cornell University asked over 1,200 elderly Americans about their regrets in life.[9] Researchers expected to hear stories about careers, relationship decisions, parenting decisions, financial decisions, or other "big" life decisions.

The researchers were surprised by the responses because they heard the same thing over and over from many different people of many diverse backgrounds.

They wished they had not wasted so much of their life worrying. They regretted worrying their life away.

Have you ever calculated how much time you spend worrying?

Many of us spend multiple hours per week doing it. Add up the hours spent worrying over a lifespan, and you will discover that many of us literally waste *years* worrying.[10]

During the Creed, we consciously choose to let go of worries and give our future to God the Father who is "almighty". We profess our faith that the risen Jesus who we encounter at Mass in the words of the Bible and in the Eucharist is fully God and gives us a reason to hope no matter how many reasons we have to worry. The Creed leads us to follow the faithful generations of Christians before us who relied on God's divine help in their lives. The Creed prepares us for the Liturgy of the Eucharist when Jesus will unite us to himself and channel divine life into our souls.

The Creed uses the image of "light from light" to refer to how

Jesus and God the Father both share in the same divine life. The image of a candle being lit from another candle without diminishing the light of the original candle has been used by the Church for centuries in the Creed to describe how God the Son has always shared in the same divine nature as God the Father without diminishing his majesty or power. Because Jesus, the Son of God, is "consubstantial" with the Father, we come in contact with the true substance of God when we encounter Jesus during the Mass. The Creed recognizes the paradox of God being majestic, mysterious, and transcendent. And also, at the same time humble, accessible, and near.

While praying the Creed, we bow during the words that emphasize the humility of the Son of God who came down from heaven "and by the Holy Spirit was incarnate of the Virgin Mary, and became man." Our bow is a physical way for us to show reverential gratitude towards the Son of God who lowered himself to enter into the brokenness of our world filled with sin, so that he might lift us up to share in God's life through the transforming power of the Holy Spirit that is now working through the Church. The same invisible presence of the Holy Spirit that was at work in the Incarnation is at work in our lives today, especially through the sacraments of the Church and the Christian community.

Our praying of the Creed during Mass is our way of admitting that we are not God and that we need God's help in our lives. In admitting we are not God, we are also acknowledging that we cannot fix everyone else's problems either. We are confessing that much of our worrying is a futile attempt to be in control of what ultimately lies beyond our control.

The practical advice of Saint Francis de Sales summarizes what it means to let go of our worries and believe in God's care for us:

> Do not think about what will happen tomorrow, for the
> same eternal Father who takes care of you today

will look out for you tomorrow and always. Either he will keep you from evil or he will give you invincible courage to endure it.[11]

THE UNIVERSAL PRAYER

...We pray to the Lord.
Lord, hear our prayer.

"It's not just about you."

When I was a small child, my mother would take me and my older brother to visit an elderly woman at a local nursing home.

One beautiful summer day, my mother announced that we needed to end playtime in our backyard to prepare to make a visit to the nursing home. I was not thrilled. A feisty, red-headed child with a streak of stubbornness in me, I began to complain and lament. I did not want to stop playing and I ranted about how I did not like going to the nursing home. I tried to drive home my argument with the comprehensive assertion that I hated everything about the nursing home, especially the unique smell of the place. I *really* hated the smell of the nursing home.

My mother's reply was quite simple: "It's not just about you."

She then patiently explained that the reason we went to the nursing home was because Hazel had no family to visit her. Mom further pointed out that we were the only kids who ever visited Hazel and that our short, 15-minute visits were the high-light of her month. The reason we were going to the nursing home was not because it was fun or because we were getting something out of it ourselves, but to share love with someone else.

"It's not just about you."

The same could be said of why we show up and pray at Mass. It is not just about us. It is not just so that we will "get something out of it" ourselves. Part of why we are at Mass is to share love with other people, to help other people.

Even our simple presence at Mass can be a way of helping others. Over the years, many people at my parishes have shared with me that they are inspired by the sacrifices others make to be at Mass. As a priest, I often look out at the congregation and find my faith bolstered by the people in the pews. Some elderly folks can barely hear or see, but they come to Mass anyway. Young parents go to large amounts of work to get their small children ready for Mass, knowing that their kids will interrupt their reflection many times throughout the Mass. But they come anyway. Many people work long shifts all week as doctors in hospitals, as school teachers in classrooms, as laborers in factories, as stay-at-home parents, and in other exhausting roles. An extra hour or two of sleep on Sunday morning would be very helpful to them, but they choose to attend Mass anyway.

Never underestimate the power of the witness you give by going to Mass. Other people are watching. Other people are lifted up by your presence and supported by the prayers you offer during Mass, even when you have spent half the Mass corralling your children in a pew, or struggling to understand a priest from a foreign country with a thick accent, or trying to sing along with a folk group that really should just retire.

The Prayer of the Faithful at Mass makes it clear that we do not go to the Mass simply for our individual benefit. The prayers we offer at the Mass serve others. They help others experience God's grace in their lives.

The Prayer of the Faithful is also called the "Universal Prayer". These prayers of petition usually involve a deacon or reader reciting short descriptions of various needs to which the congregation responds "Lord, hear our prayer!"

There can be times during Mass when we are fixated on our own needs, our own desires, our own preferences, our own fears, our own problems. The Prayer of the Faithful pushes us outside that limited world to pray for the needs of others.

The petitions are "universal" because they focus our attention beyond the borders of our daily routine and orient us towards the need all people have for God's saving help in their lives. The Prayer of the Faithful typically includes petitions for the universal Church, public authorities and leaders of nations, people in situations of grave need elsewhere in the world, as well as the greater local community.

The placement of the Prayer of the Faithful after our encounter with God's Word is significant. These prayers are a response to the challenge the Word of God consistently echoes in our ears to look beyond ourselves and to be attentive to the needs of others.[12] The Universal Prayer is the proper response to the command of Jesus telling us to be Good Samaritans who love "our neighbor", who is ultimately anyone is need (Luke 10:29-37).

During the Universal Prayer, ask yourself: Who else needs my prayers today? And then pray for them.

The Prayer of the Faithful reawakens our awareness of our Christian obligation to serve the poor and look out for the most vulnerable members of the human family. The prayers we offer at Mass should naturally lead us to be more generous, caring, and helpful to persons in need.

The Universal Prayer concludes the Liturgy of the Word and Mass continues with the Liturgy of the Eucharist. The Preparation of the Gifts and the Eucharistic Prayer will lead us further beyond ourselves, directing our attention firmly on God the Father, uniting us to Jesus' sacrifice, and allowing the Holy Spirit to bring us into closer relationships with other people we are called to love and serve.

THE LITURGY OF
THE EUCHARIST

THE PREPARATION
OF THE GIFTS

The Priest:
Blessed are you, Lord God of all creation,
for through your goodness we have received
the bread we offer you:
fruit of the earth and work of human hands,
it will become for us the bread of life.
The people:
Blessed be God for ever.

When I was 22 years old, I began volunteering in a soup kitchen operated by Mother Teresa's sisters, the Missionaries of Charity, in Rome. After a couple of months, one of the sisters asked me to be an altar server for a Mass when some sisters would make their final vows.

The Mass began as usual with the readings and homily, and then the sisters made their promises of poverty, chastity, and obedience to serve the poorest of the poor. The sisters promised to live these vows following the radical example of generosity Mother Teresa embodied during her life.

After the vows, as Mass continued, something very striking took place. Instead of an ordinary offertory procession with people carrying forward a container (cruet) of wine and a gold dish (ciborium) filled with hosts, something special occurred. Each of the sisters who had made their vows walked down the aisle carrying one small host. Arriving near the altar, they placed the tiny, white pieces of bread into the gold dish, which was then placed on the altar where the bread would be consecrated to become the real presence of Jesus, the Eucharist.

A commentator explained that the single host each woman carried symbolized her life she was offering entirely to God. Each woman was offering to God her gifts, her talents, her strengths, her weaknesses, her sinfulness, her past, her future, her hopes, and her dreams. They were giving their entire selves, their whole lives, to Jesus, so that they could be united completely to him who gave his life revealing God's love for the world.

The women were offering their lives to God, so that they would be blessed and consecrated along with the bread and the wine to make the love of Jesus present in the world.

The same dynamic is present at every Mass. Each Mass is an opportunity for each of us to offer our lives to God. As Jesus unites our lives to his during the Mass, daily life takes on new meaning and becomes a place where Jesus' love is revealed in the world.

Members of a parish bring forward bread and wine in a procession at Mass to express that we are all offering to God the fruit of our labors and all our activity from the past week.[13] This moment at Sunday Mass is a time to think back on the past week and consciously offer all our actions from the past week to God. We offer God our successes and all the moments when we did God's work and were faithful to our vocations. We also offer to God our sins and failures, so Jesus can redeem us, purify us, and transform us in the same way that he transformed the greatest mistake and failure ever (humanity's choice to crucify him) into something beautiful (the resurrection).

When we recognize that even the mundane moments of our week can be offered to God at the Mass, these then take on greater significance. Even the most tedious, unexciting, and laborious moments of any day can be offered to God at the Mass. These moments become special and profound as Jesus accepts our offering and lifts them up into the sacrifice of his life that he offered to give glory to God and bring salvation to the whole world.

At the beginning of each day, remind yourself that all your actions that day will be part of the offering you make to God at Mass, and this offering will be united to Jesus' sacrifice which gives glory to God and brings salvation to others.

After the altar is prepared, the priest lifts up the bread and then the wine, while praying short prayers adapted from the Passover ritual that Jesus would have prayed during the Last Supper. These prayers talk about how we are offering to God both what we have received through God's goodness as well as our own labors, the "work of human hands". The bread and wine symbolize our self-offering to God and prepare us to participate through the Eucharistic Prayer in Jesus' self-offering of himself to the Father.

The Preparation of the Gifts is a time of preparation. To prepare to make a total gift of self to God in the Eucharistic Prayer. To offer anything less, would be a missed opportunity.

By the Mystery...and the Prayer over the Offerings

The Deacon or the Priest:
By the mystery of this water and wine
may we come to share in the divinity of Christ
who humbled himself to share in our humanity.
The Priest:
Blessed are you, Lord God of all creation,
for through your goodness we have received
the wine we offer you:
fruit of the vine and work of human hands,
it will become our spiritual drink.
The people:
Blessed be God for ever.
The Priest:
With humble spirit and contrite heart
may we be accepted by you, O Lord,
and may our sacrifice in your sight this day
be pleasing to you, Lord God.

Wash me, O Lord, from my iniquity
and cleanse me from my sin.
The Priest:
Pray, brothers and sisters,
that my sacrifice and yours
may be acceptable to God,
the almighty Father.
The people:
May the Lord accept the sacrifice at your hands
for the praise and glory of his name,
for our good
and the good of all his holy Church.
The Priest:
The Prayer over the Offerings...
The people:
Amen.

"Father, they do that so the priest does not get drunk!"

A few years ago, I was visiting a sixth-grade religion classroom at Most Blessed Sacrament Parish in Toledo and teaching the students about the meaning of the rituals of the Mass. When I was explaining the offertory procession and the preparation of the altar before the Eucharistic Prayer, I asked the students if they had ever noticed that the priest or deacon pours a few drops of water into the chalice after filling it with wine.

A good number of the students were altar servers and acknowledged that they had seen this done many times. So, I asked them: "Do you know *why* we add a little bit of water to the wine?"

One of the boys quickly raised his hand in the air with an eager facial expression that said: "Pick me, pick me! I know the answer!"

I called on this enthusiastic student and asked him to explain the deep meaning behind the ancient Christian tradition of adding a few drops of water to the cup of wine during the Mass.

The boy eagerly responded: "Father, they do that so the priest does not get drunk at Mass!"

Most of the heads of the other students nodded up and down as if to say in agreement: "Yes, that really makes sense. It would be a problem if father was tipsy during Mass."

Historically, adding water to the wine in the priest's chalice has been part of the ritual of the Mass from the early days of Christianity. However, the reason we do this today is not because of worries about the priest getting drunk during Mass. Important teachers in the early Church, like St. Cyprian in the third century, were already then emphasizing that these drops of water have significant theological meaning.[14]

The wine in the chalice that will soon be blessed and consecrated represents the divinity of God. The drops of water represent our humanity. Water uniting with the wine represents how Jesus united our humanity with God's divinity and made it possible for us to be closely united to God as we live human life here on earth.

Just as the drops of water poured into the chalice become united with the wine, so too are we united closely to God, especially through Baptism and reception of Holy Communion.

When the priest pours the water into the chalice at Mass, he quietly says: "By the mystery of this water and wine may we come to share in the divinity of Christ who humbled himself to share in our humanity."

These words of the Mass remind us that God desires a deep, lasting friendship with us. They emphasize that the Son of God chose to enter into human life, so that he could raise us up to share in the everlasting life of the persons of the Trinity. St. Athanasius once said: "The Son of God became man, so that he might make us what he is."[15]

The Incarnation of the Son of God in human flesh proves to us that there is Someone who knows our weakness and imperfection, and still chooses to love us anyway. God desires to be associated with us even though we may feel we are sometimes a disappointment to God or to others. In fact, the mingling of the water and wine at Mass remind us of God's desire to lift us up to be able to live our human life at a higher level.

Again, the Son of God became what we are, so that he might make us what he is. Jesus can help us become what he is and help us become more loving, patient, merciful, truthful, generous, and courageous.

Jesus can build us up with divine courage and hope when fear and worry threaten to overwhelm us. Jesus can provide divine wisdom and patience when strong temptations to judge others or gossip confront us. Jesus can fill us with divine generosity and mercy when we have to deal with people whose arrogance, selfishness, and greed frustrate us. Jesus can give us a peace that is not the result of having a perfect life or a life free of problems or pain, but rather, a peace that comes from knowing that we are not alone, that we are loved, and that our life is headed in the right direction.

Jesus is leading us in the right direction. Leading us towards a better life. Leading us through our participation in the Mass to the divine life of heaven.

The Preparation of the Gifts is a time when we give God permission to lead us into the future according to his plans. We follow Jesus' lead, we enter into his self-surrender to the Father that characterized the entirety of his life, including the Last Supper when betrayal, suffering, and death were looming.

After the priest has prayed the short prayers from the Passover with the bread and the wine, then he bows at the altar and quietly says: "With humble spirit and contrite heart may we be accepted by you, O Lord, and may our sacrifice in your sight this day be pleasing to you, Lord God."

These words are paraphrased from the Book of Daniel in the Old Testament. In chapter 3 of the Book of Daniel, a ruthless, pagan leader threw three men into a fire. He wanted to kill these men because they were faithful to God, refusing to offer sacrifice to pagan idols. One of the men in the fire prayed fervently for himself and on behalf of the other men. In his prayer, Azariah offered their lives to God and entrusted their future to divine providence.

God answered his prayer by miraculously saving these faithful men.

The priest quietly prays the words of Azariah during the Mass, offering his life to God along with the lives of everyone participating in the Mass. Azariah's prayer leads him to trust that God will act in the lives of his people who, like the men in the Book of Daniel, offer themselves and their future to God.

The priest speaks many of the prayers during the Preparation of the Altar quietly, especially when the congregation is singing a hymn or chant. However, the priest always prays out loud the words: "Pray, brothers and sisters, that my sacrifice and yours may be acceptable to God, the almighty Father." These words and the people's response reinforce our awareness that we are all offering our lives together to God at the altar. The optional use of incense during the Preparation of the Gifts creates rising clouds of smoke, which symbolize our prayers and the offering of our lives ascending through Jesus to God the Father during the Eucharistic Prayer.[16]

The Prayer over the Offerings comes immediately before the Eucharistic Prayer. This prayer acknowledges the offering we are making of our lives to God and asks that God, in his great mercy, might accept this offering. Our need for mercy as we approach the Eucharistic Prayer is also expressed by the washing of the priest's hands shortly before the beginning of the Eucharistic Prayer.[17] The priest prays: "Wash me, O Lord, from my iniquity and cleanse me from my sin." As sinners, we do not deserve to be united with God, yet because of God's incredible mercy towards us, we are able to experience intimacy with the Trinity at the Mass. Undeserving as we are, Jesus leads us into the divine life of the Trinity through the Eucharistic Prayer.

THE EUCHARISTIC PRAYER

THE THANKSGIVING

The Priest:
The Lord be with you.
The people:
And with your spirit.
The Priest:
Lift up your hearts.
The people:
We lift them up to the Lord.
The Priest:
Let us give thanks to the Lord our God.
The people:
It is right and just.
The Priest:
The Preface…

What was he giving thanks for?

During every Mass, the priest repeats Jesus' words from the Last Supper: "Jesus took bread and, *giving thanks*, broke it, and gave it to his disciples, saying . . .this is my body" and then the priest takes the chalice and says that Jesus "*once more giving thanks. . .gave it to his disciples, saying . . .this is the chalice of my blood*".

On the night before he died, Jesus chose *to give thanks.*

Have you ever stopped to think about what Jesus was giving thanks for at the Last Supper?

After all, it was a rather stressful, upsetting time in his life. Serious tension had been building at the end of Jesus' ministry. An influential group of people had been looking for an opportunity to kill him. Among Jesus' closest friends at table with him that evening was a man (Judas) who would betray him for 30 pieces of silver.

It was one of the most difficult days of Jesus' life. The tension would become so great that he would sweat blood during his agony in the Garden of Gethsemane later that evening.

And yet, that evening, Jesus still *gave thanks.*

Giving thanks for what?

One clue as to why Jesus was giving thanks is found in the Old Testament. The Book of Exodus narrates the origins of the Jewish Passover, which was the meal Jesus and his disciples celebrated at the Last Supper (Exodus 12:1-28).

The people of Israel celebrated the first ever Passover meal on the night before God powerfully manifested his love for them by freeing them from slavery in Egypt.

After this saving event in Egypt, the people of Israel repeated the Passover meal on a yearly basis to remember and give thanks for God's saving love during this Exodus event. The yearly Passover meal gave the people a chance to express thanks for the ways they had continued to experience God's saving love during the past year.

However, the Passover celebration was not just about the past. It was also about today. And the future. The Jewish people believed that during their annual celebration of the Passover, God was giving them a special opportunity to experience the same saving love at work in the original Exodus event. The Jewish people celebrated with the understanding that the same God who intervened in the lives of Jewish slaves in Egypt would make his saving love available to them during their Passover ritual. This ritual was a way of allowing God's saving love into their lives. And furthermore, the celebration of the Passover included a prayer of gratitude for ways God would intervene in their lives in the future.

By choosing to celebrate the Passover on the evening of the Last Supper, Jesus was choosing to give thanks for God the Father's love in his own life. As a devout Jewish man, Jesus gave thanks during the Last Supper for all the ways he had experienced God the Father's love in his humanity during the past year. Jesus also asked the Father's saving intervention in his current situation of stress, turmoil, and anguish. Additionally, Jesus gave thanks for God's intervention in his future.

In other words, Jesus gave thanks ahead of time for God the Father's saving intervention in his future, his resurrection, that would make it possible for us to share in the life of heaven. During the Passover Jesus was giving thanks for God the Father's love that would *seem* so distant and absent during the darkness of Good Friday, yet was still deeply at work then and would fully be manifest a few days later on Easter Sunday.

Jesus, on the night before he died, gave thanks that God the Father's saving love would bring us salvation through his suffering and death on the cross. Jesus was giving thanks that his death and resurrection would make it possible for humanity to pass over from bondage under the reign of sin to the freedom of God's Kingdom of holiness. Jesus was giving thanks that God the Father would free us from sin and make it possible for us to enjoy a close relationship with him forever.

In other words, on the night before he died, Jesus gave thanks for you and me.

It can be tempting to think of Jesus dying only for "humanity" in general, and yet, the Bible emphasizes time and time again that the Son of God died for *me*. The Son of God died for you. The Son of God loved us as unique individuals, and not just as one big giant blob of humanity (see Galatians 2:20).

For example, at the Last Supper, Jesus took time to wash the dirty feet of each apostle to reveal his personal love for each of us. He loves us completely and totally "to the end" (John 13:1). Later that same evening, praying to the Father, he referred to us, his disciples, as God the Father's "gift" to him (John 17:24).

Jesus considered us (his disciples) as a "gift" worth giving thanks for during the Last Supper. Jesus was grateful for us and gave thanks for the gift that we are to him on the night before he died! Jesus gave thanks for God the Father's saving love that would allow us to spend eternity with him in heaven.

When we gather for Mass, the priest invites us to have the same attitude as Jesus during the Passover celebration in which he celebrated his Last Supper and instituted the Eucharist. The priest says: "Let us give thanks to the Lord our God."

And the people respond: "It is right and just."

Like Jesus on the night of the Last Supper and like the people of Israel before the Exodus event, we too have plenty of stress in our lives. We have plenty of problems and trials. And yet, Jesus invites us to enter into his prayer of thanksgiving to God the Father for the many ways his saving love is working in our lives. We lift up our hearts, focusing our attention on the Giver of all good gifts.

Following this invitation to gratitude, the priest prays the "Preface" of the Eucharistic Prayer. The Preface is the beginning of the Eucharistic Prayer in which we "lift up our hearts to the Lord" by focusing on God and what God has done in salvation history. The Preface primarily focuses on thanking God for his loving interventions throughout salvation history in the lives of his people.[18]

The Preface is an opportunity to count our own blessings and thank God for them. To make the most of this moment, spend some time before Mass making a "gratitude list" of blessings, both big and small, from the past week. Then during the Preface, consciously call to mind these blessings, thanking God the Father for them.

Some blessings can be easy to overlook. They may not seem like blessings in the moment. Some of the times when God was closest to us were moments of difficulty, heartbreak, sadness, grief, loss, sickness, or other painful challenges. It is especially important during this part of the Mass to give thanks for God's help in moments of suffering, since we are uniting our thanksgiving with Jesus who on the night of the Last Supper gave thanks for God's faithful love that would quietly accompany him in his suffering.

On the night before he died, Jesus gave thanks for his suffering, his pain, his agony, and the betrayal he experienced. Jesus gave thanks for the opportunity to share love in these dark moments. He gave thanks for the good that God the Father would bring out of his sufferings, even though, at the time, they would seem to be a divine curse and signs the Father had abandoned him.

No matter how terrible our week has been or how intimidating the pain of the week ahead will be, the Mass invites us to give thanks to the Lord our God. We give thanks not because we perfectly understand God's plan or because we see clearly how God will use our suffering to bring about good.

We give thanks as an act of faith. We give thanks ahead of time.

For several decades in the 20th century, huge crowds of people daily sought out a humble, Franciscan friar in Detroit, Michigan for counsel and spiritual advice. From affluent business executives to penniless beggars, long lines of people from all walks of life waited each day to visit with Father Solanus Casey to hear his words of wisdom and to pray with him. Father Casey's reputation as a man of tremendous spiritual insight, coupled with his reputation as a miracle worker, led thousands to seek his guidance.

Time and time again his advice was the same: "Give thanks ahead of time". Father Casey, now Blessed Solanus Casey, encouraged people to take their petitions to God with gratitude already on their lips, trusting that God is at work long before they see any results.

At every Mass, we enter into the prayer of Jesus at the Last Supper who gave thanks ahead of time. At Mass, our prayer of thanksgiving is united to Jesus, who strengthens our belief in God's power to bring good out of our suffering, even when we struggle to see how this is possible. At Mass, we take time to be grateful not just for what God has done in the past, but also for what God will do in the future. Gratitude is the underlying theme of the entire Eucharistic Prayer.

THE ACCLAMATION

Holy, Holy, Holy Lord God of hosts.
Heaven and earth are full of your glory.
Hosanna in the highest.
Blessed is he who comes in the name of the Lord.
Hosanna in the highest.

Will heaven be boring?

When teaching theology classes to college students, I would often ask them what images first came to mind when they thought about heaven.

Their answers were usually the same: angels with wings dressed in white gowns floating among clouds. Deceased persons existing in a sort of blissful, dream-like state also floating with these angels among the clouds.

My follow up question was always the same: Do you really want to spend all of eternity in that situation? Wouldn't spending an endless eternity floating among clouds eventually become boring?

Most students would admit they feared that heaven might become dull and unexciting. Living here on earth seemed more exciting than what they imagined heaven to be like.

The last book of the New Testament, the Book of Revelation, records a vision the apostle John had of what heaven will be like (see Revelation 4 and following).

As John attempts to describe the inexpressible glory of heaven, what he depicts is not a scene of isolated souls and angels aimlessly floating among clouds. Rather, a multitude of angelic beings and human persons united together in celebration.

This great community of believers was a group of tremendous diversity, "from every nation, race, people and tongue" (Revelation 7:9). Their oneness had not dissolved the uniqueness of the individuals gathered there. The people John sees in heaven are fully alive in all their uniqueness yet bonded together into one family of love.

This vision of the Book of Revelation is telling us that heaven is not an anonymous "one-size-fits-all" sort of existence. Heaven is an existence in which we are both fully ourselves in all our uniqueness and also deeply immersed within a meaningful community. In heaven, we will be able to live deep and meaningful relationships with other people in true harmony and authentic love. These relationships will be characterized by trust. In heaven, the insecurities and fears that burden our relationships here on earth will be gone, and we will be able to experience each other in freedom and peace.[19]

Another central theme of John's vision of heaven is the image of the Son of God as a shepherd. This is also a prevalent theme in the gospel of John. Jesus said his goal as the Good Shepherd is to give us abundant life, to give us eternal life, to help us to become fully alive. He said: "I came so that they might have life and have it more abundantly" (John 10:10). We will experience this fullness of abundant life in heaven.

The Book of Revelation makes clear that eternal life with God in heaven will be a fulfilling life. Every hunger and thirst will be satisfied (Revelation 21:1-7). This includes the most significant desires of our hearts: the desire to love and to be loved, to be appreciated, to be noticed, to be close to others, to be safe and secure, to experience peace and joy, to be part of something bigger than ourselves. Jesus, the Good Shepherd is leading us to a life in heaven where our deepest longings are finally fulfilled.[20]

In heaven, we will experience the truth about who God is. We will see how good and loving God really is. We will be able see how much God loves us. We will be overwhelmed by the beauty of God and recognize the beauty the Creator placed on the earth, the beauty of other people, the beauty of ourselves, and the beauty of the life we lived on earth. In heaven, we will be over-whelmed with the joy and happiness of basking in God's truth, beauty, and goodness without any effects of sin hindering us.

Our existence in heaven will be fuller and more exciting than any moment of earthly life. Eternal life with God in heaven will be more exhilarating than the thrill of all our experiences on earth combined. Good times here are just a foretaste of the fullness of life in heaven. Our experiences of goodness, truth, beauty, happiness, meaning, and fulfillment are just small pre-views of what we will enjoy in heaven.[21] Heaven will not be boring because we will constantly be discovering more of God's goodness.

As we sing the "Holy, Holy, Holy" (in Latin: "*Sanctus*") during the Mass, we are anticipating our experience of God's glory in heaven. In heaven, we will see with clarity how heaven and earth are full of God's glory. We will see how God's awesomeness goes beyond human comprehension, human words, and human designs.

The Book of Revelation describes angels in heaven relishing in the privilege of being in the presence of God. "Day and night they do not stop exclaiming: "Holy, holy, holy is the Lord God al-mighty, who was, and who is, and who is to come"" (Revelation 4:8). These words of the angels in heaven are the words we chant during the "Sanctus" at Mass.

In the Old Testament, the prophet Isaiah described a vision of God's glory in heaven, which also included angels chanting the Sanctus: ""Holy, holy, holy is the LORD of hosts!" they cried one to the other. "All the earth is filled with his glory!"" (Isaiah 6:3).

During the Mass, we unite our voices with the angels in heaven who use the word "holy" to describe the fullness of life that the three persons of the Blessed Trinity share in heaven.[22]

The Mass, in a very real way, inserts us into the heavenly cele-bration of God's greatness. Our participation at the Mass draws us up into the celebration of heaven. "By the Eucharistic cele-bration we already unite ourselves with the heavenly liturgy and anticipate eternal life when God will be all in all".[23]

The words of the Preface that introduce the "Sanctus" under-line the connection between the Mass and heaven. A common conclusion to Preface states: "And so, with the Angels and the Saints we declare your glory, as with one voice we acclaim: Holy, Holy, Holy, Lord God of hosts..."

Some other prefaces contain an even more elaborate descrip-tion of the community of heaven that we are entering into during the Mass. For example, the conclusion from Preface I of the Most Holy Eucharist states: "And so, with Angels and Arch-angels, with Thrones and Dominions, and with all the hosts and Powers of heaven, we sing the hymn of your glory, as without end we acclaim: Holy, Holy, Lord God of hosts..."

Archangels, Thrones, and Dominions are classic Christian cat-egories used to differentiate the various groups of angels who share in God's life in heaven. The word "hosts" in the Sanc-tus ("Lord God of hosts") was used in the ancient world to de-scribe large groups of soldiers making up an army.[24] During the Sanctus, the praising of God as "Lord God of hosts" is an acknowledgement of the great multitude of angels and saints, God's army, who are already celebrating God's ultimate victory over the forces of evil that are at work in the world. We join their worship of the Trinity through the Sanctus.

The final phrases of the Sanctus find their Biblical origin in the shouts of the crowds who greeted Jesus as he made his tri-umphal entry into Jerusalem to celebrate the Passover with his disciples, and then to die on the cross for our salvation. The crowds shouted out: "Hosanna to the Son of David; blessed is he who comes in the name of the Lord; hosanna in the highest" (Matthew 21:9).

The crowds did not spontaneously invent this acclamation on their own, but rather, they were quoting Psalm 118. Devout Jews chanted Psalm 118 to praise God and to ask God to give them a Messiah who would bring them salvation. The word "Hosanna" is a request begging God: "Save!", "Give Salvation!". [25] Thus, the crowds chanting the words of Psalm 118:25-26 as Jesus en-tered Jerusalem were praising God and asking for God's saving intervention through Jesus, the Messiah. These words are most appropriate for us to chant during Mass as we welcome the saving effects of Jesus' death and resurrection into our own lives through the Eucharistic Prayer and the Rite of Communion. We acknowledge that God who is seated on the highest throne above all creatures, chooses to be near us and to help us.

THE FIRST EPICLESIS

The Priest:
Eucharistic Prayer II:
You are indeed Holy, O Lord,
the fount of all holiness.
Make holy, therefore, these gifts, we pray,
by sending down your Spirit upon them like the dewfall,
so that they may become for us
the Body and + Blood of our Lord Jesus Christ.

Eucharistic Prayer III:
You are indeed Holy, O Lord,
and all you have created
rightly gives you praise,
for through your Son our Lord Jesus Christ,
by the power and working of the Holy Spirit,
you give life to all things and make them holy,
and you never cease to gather a people to yourself,
so that from the rising of the sun to its setting
a pure sacrifice may be offered to your name.

Therefore, O Lord, we humbly implore you:
by the same Spirit graciously make holy
these gifts we have brought to you for consecration,
that they may become the Body and + Blood
of your Son our Lord Jesus Christ,
at whose command we celebrate these mysteries.

In the year 2010, the Vatican published an updated English translation of the Mass. This is why we now say "and with your spirit" rather than "and also with you" as the response to the priest saying "The Lord be with you". In the Creed, we now say that God the Son was "consubstantial" with the Father, whereas before we said that the Son was "one in being with the Father". And so on.

I was living in Rome during the time when many of the meetings took place to decide which words should be used in the new translation. Every now and again, we would hear rumors about what the translators had supposedly discussed at those meetings.

One story I heard was about a discussion that allegedly took place about Eucharistic Prayer II. The final translation now reads: "Make holy, therefore, these gifts, we pray, by sending down your Spirit upon them like the dewfall, so that they may become for us the Body and Blood of our Lord Jesus Christ".

As the story goes, the committee of experts (linguists, theologians, bishops, etc.) received a draft translation of this prayer that read: "send down your Spirit upon them like the *mountain dew*".

Experts from the United States at the meeting stepped in and made it clear that mentioning "mountain dew" during the Eucharistic Prayer was not going to help people think about the Holy Spirit. Instead, people at Mass in the USA would be thinking of green, carbonated soda pop loaded with caffeine and sugar if the words "mountain dew" were spoken at Mass.

And so, we ended up with a translation that reads "like the dewfall" instead.

I don't know if this actually took place during the meeting of experts, but as I was hearing this story I realized that I had no idea what the connection was between the Holy Spirit and dew?

In the Old Testament world, dew was something very special and mysterious (See Psalm 133:3; Isaiah 26:19, 45:8; Hosea 14:5-6). We have to remember that people back then did not have the meteorological knowledge of today. They did not have the scientific understanding of condensation, humidity, dew points, and the water cycle as we do.

So in the morning, when the dew appeared on the ground, it

seemed to come out of nowhere. Its source was mysterious and invisible. The much-welcomed dew seemed to have miraculous origins.

Dew was incredibly important in the Middle Eastern world for refreshment. It nurtured life, providing a significant portion of the moisture plants need for survival. Dew made life possible in an area where rainfall was sparse and infrequent.

In the Old Testament, when the people of Israel were traveling from slavery in Egypt through the wilderness to the Promised Land, the morning dewfall provided refreshment. In fact, God gave the people special food, manna, along with the morning dew. The dewfall brought them nourishment and strength for their journey (Exodus 16:13-15).

This is why at Mass we ask God's Spirit to come like the dewfall. We are asking for God's invisible, miraculous, and mysterious presence to come out of nowhere and provide us with the spiritual refreshment and nourishment we need for our journey to the Promised Land of heaven. We ask the invisible Holy Spirit to come down and provide us with the food of the Eucharist that will fill us with life.

While the imagery of the dewfall is not used in every Eucharistic Prayer, there is a section in each of the Eucharistic Prayers invoking God to miraculously transform the offerings on the altar into the Body and Blood of Jesus Christ. The Greek word *epiclesis* describes this powerful moment in the Mass when the Holy Spirit is called down from on high to transform the humble offerings we have placed on the altar.[26]

Over the centuries, many forms of Church architecture have expressed the importance of this moment by placing an image of the Holy Spirit directly above the altar to provide a visual reminder of the unseen, transforming power of the Holy Spirit during the Mass. In some European churches, there is a canopy (*baldacchino*) over the altar to direct the minds of the faithful to the transforming work of the Holy Spirit in the Eucharistic Prayer.

During this portion of the Mass, the faithful kneel in reverential awe, as God's power is invisibly at work in their midst. This is a time during the Mass to take a deep breath and acknowledge that God's work is not always visible or immediately apparent to our human eyes. God is much closer to us than we can see!

THE INSTITUTION NARRATIVE AND CONSECRATION

The Priest:
Eucharistic Prayer II:
At the time he was betrayed
and entered willingly into his Passion,
he took bread and, giving thanks, broke it,
and gave it to his disciples, saying:

TAKE THIS, ALL OF YOU, AND EAT OF IT,
FOR THIS IS MY BODY,
WHICH WILL BE GIVEN UP FOR YOU.

In a similar way, when supper was ended,
he took the chalice
and, once more giving thanks,
he gave it to his disciples, saying:

TAKE THIS, ALL OF YOU, AND DRINK FROM IT,
FOR THIS IS THE CHALICE OF MY BLOOD,
THE BLOOD OF THE NEW AND ETERNAL COVENANT,
WHICH WILL BE POURED OUT FOR YOU AND FOR
*　MANY*
FOR THE FORGIVENESS OF SINS.
DO THIS IN MEMORY OF ME.

Eucharistic Prayer III:
For on the night he was betrayed

he himself took bread,
and, giving you thanks, he said the blessing,
broke the bread and gave it to his disciples, saying:

TAKE THIS, ALL OF YOU, AND EAT OF IT,
FOR THIS IS MY BODY,
WHICH WILL BE GIVEN UP FOR YOU.

In a similar way, when supper was ended,
he took the chalice,
and, giving you thanks, he said the blessing,
and gave the chalice to his disciples, saying:

TAKE THIS, ALL OF YOU, AND DRINK FROM IT,
FOR THIS IS THE CHALICE OF MY BLOOD,
THE BLOOD OF THE NEW AND ETERNAL COVENANT,
WHICH WILL BE POURED OUT FOR YOU AND FOR
    MANY
FOR THE FORGIVENESS OF SINS.
DO THIS IN MEMORY OF ME.

What are you living your life for?

The answer to this question is complicated.

Often, people are doing some of what they do every day for the sake of making more money to buy more things like new furniture, clothing, an SUV, or a bigger home.

What they are doing every day may be for the sake of achieving greater popularity, social status, or power in the eyes of those who live nearby, hang out with them, or observe their posts on social media.

It also may be for the sake of "success". Success in maintaining their health and physical beauty. Success in relationships. Success in the corporate world. Often, much is sacrificed for the sake of success.

Further, it may be for the sake of pleasure. Seeking more intense pleasure, they are willing sometimes even to sacrifice their safety, health, or other relationships to experience the thrill of pleasure, as well as, the escape from reality it provides.

Finally, it may be for the sake of others. Making donations for the destitute. Sacrificing their time for friends who need to talk about problems. Using their energy for the sake of bringing happiness to a spouse, special friend, family member, children, or even random strangers.

What are you living for?

The words Jesus spoke during the Last Supper teach us how he would answer this question.

Jesus lived his life *for* us. Jesus gave himself completely and totally *for* us and *for* our salvation.

Jesus said "this is my body which will be given up *for* you...this is the chalice of my blood...which will be poured out *for* you and *for* many *for* the forgiveness of sins".

We refer to these special words as the "Institution Narrative" because Jesus used these words during the Last Supper to institute the Eucharist.

Simply put, the Institution Narrative are words that tell us how much God loves us. Jesus speaks these words to us through the voice of the priest during Mass to tell us how important we are to him. We are so important to him that he sacrificed his life for us on a cross.

All of what Jesus did during his life on earth was not for the sake of becoming wealthy or achieving popularity, social status, or power. Jesus did not dedicate his energy to being "successful" nor did he make pleasure the motivating factor of his choices. He chose to sacrifice all of that for the sake of loving us in the most radical and complete way possible.

Jesus did what he did each day out of love for us. Long days of travel to countless towns and villages. Teaching the truth. Forgiving sins. Forming a community. Everything he did was dedicated to building an unbreakable bond of friendship, a covenant, between humanity and God that would last forever. His thoughts, words, and energy were directed towards us and focused on bringing about the lasting covenant with us that God the Father had planned.

The directives that instruct priests how to perform the rituals of the Mass emphasize that the words of the Institution Narrative are some of the most special words the priest prays during the Mass. The rubrics in *The Roman Missal* insist that during the Instruction Narrative, "the words of the Lord should be pronounced clearly and distinctly, as the nature of these words require".

The words of the Institution Narrative are extremely special words because at Mass Jesus speaks these words to each of us and solemnly declares his love for us.

Jesus originally spoke these words in the context of a Passover celebration, which was an opportunity for people to renew their commitment to their covenant relationship with God. The Mass continues this dynamic as Jesus reassures us through the words of the Institution Narrative that he will always love us with the same divine love that motivated him to sacrifice his life for us on the cross.

The words of the Institution Narrative could be described as God's wedding vows to humanity, since Jesus spoke these words as a promise of his unconditional love, his covenant commitment to us. In a certain sense, we could say that through the words of the Institution Narrative, Jesus is renewing his wedding vows to humanity during each Mass.

We choose to renew our own commitment to this covenant through our participation at the Mass, especially as we enthusiastically say or sing the "Great Amen" at the end of the Eucharistic Prayer, giving voice to our "yes" to this everlasting covenant friendship with God.

Couples whom I have helped renew their wedding vows after several years of marriage have often shared with me that their vows meant more to them when they renewed them than when they first made them on their wedding day. Over the years of marriage, these spouses grew to know each other's strengths and weaknesses very thoroughly. Each spouse came to know the many ways he or she could be a cause of frustration and irritation to their spouse.

And yet, their spouse still chose to renew their promise to faithful love anyway! Their spouse knew well that their commitment would require sacrifice and still chose to renew this sacred promise anyway. There is something special that happens when a partner who has seen us at our worst still chooses to promise faithful love to us anyway.

Every time we participate in the Mass, Jesus renews his commitment to his covenant with us. Jesus looks into our eyes as he did to his disciples on the night of the Last Supper and promises us his faithful and merciful love. Despite the ups and downs of our relationship with him, and our sometimes wavering commitment to him, Jesus looks at us with love and says: "You are worth everything to me!"

Each time we attend Sunday Mass, Jesus reassures us that his commitment to us has not changed. He knows all the faults, sins, and selfishness we have chosen during the past week. He knows the ways we have not been faithful to him. And yet, he says to us each week: "This is my body given up for you...this is my blood shed for you...for the forgiveness of your sins".

The Catholic Church has consistently taught that the Eucharistic Prayer and the words of the Institution Narrative are much more than a simple retelling or re-enactment of the Last Supper. The Catholic Church has consistently taught that the words of the Institution Narrative describe what is actually happening to the bread and wine, as the priest, acting in the person of Jesus, says: "Take this, all of you, and eat of it, for this is my Body... Take this, all of you, and drink from it, for this is the chalice of my Blood..." The Catholic Church believes that the power of the Holy Spirit transforms the bread and wine into the real presence of Jesus' flesh and blood as the priest prays the Eucharistic Prayer during the Mass.[27]

The Catholic Church's understanding of this miracle is based on Jesus' own words during his ministry (see John 6:22-71). Jesus told the crowds:

> Amen, amen, I say to you, unless you eat the flesh of
> the Son of Man and drink his blood, you do not have life

*within you. Whoever eats my flesh and drinks my blood
has eternal life, and I will raise him on the last day. For
my flesh is true food, and my blood is true drink. Whoever eats my flesh and drinks my blood remains in me
and I in him (John 6:53-56).*

What happens to the bread and wine at Mass goes beyond
what human beings can accomplish on their own. God works
through the priest praying the words of the Eucharistic Prayer
and transforms the humble matter of unleavened wheat bread
and grape wine in a miracle that goes beyond anything we can
fully understand on our own.

In fact, when Jesus was teaching the people about consuming
his body and blood, the crowds argued and said, "How can this
man give us his flesh to eat?" (John 6:52). Many people in these
crowds who had accepted Jesus' other teachings stopped listening to him because they did not like this teaching about consuming his flesh and blood. Many disciples said: "This saying is hard;
who can accept it?" (John 6:60).

Jesus' response to all of their complaining was simply to encourage the people to believe what he had told them. He told
them they should not be shocked that his divine teaching goes
beyond what they had expected or what they could understand
on their own.

It is important to note that Jesus did not change or "water
down" his teaching about eating his flesh and drinking his blood
when large numbers of his disciples "returned to their former
way of life and no longer accompanied him" (John 6:66). If
he was just speaking symbolically or metaphorically, he would
have attempted to re-explain this teaching to them. Yet, he did
not do this. Jesus had meant what he had said. Jesus was teaching that eating his flesh and drinking his blood was possible and
important for our salvation.

The Catholic Church has consistently taught that the Holy
Spirit invisibly transforms the substance of the bread and wine
during Mass into the living presence of Jesus. While he is hidden from our eyes by the humble appearances of bread and

wine that remain, our belief is that through the Eucharist we encounter the same Jesus who during his earthly life taught in synagogues, healed the sick, forgave sins, carried the cross to Calvary, suffered crucifixion, rose from the dead, and ascended into heaven.

Immediately following the Institution Narrative, the priest says: "The mystery of faith", which is a fitting description of what takes place during this special moment of the Mass. The details of "how" God miraculously transforms bread and wine into the presence of Jesus are beyond human comprehension. And yet, God has clearly revealed to us the "why" behind it. God's love for us is the "why" behind the miracle of the transformation of bread and wine into the real presence of Jesus in the Eucharist. God desires to be close to us!

The Institution Narrative is a time during the Mass when we can simply enjoy the loving presence of Jesus who is near to us. This is a time to contemplate with joy the presence of Jesus who speaks to us his promise of unconditional love, reassures of his never-ending mercy towards us, and vows to dedicate himself to us for all eternity.

During the Institution Narrative, the priest purposefully pauses and holds up the large host after saying the words "This is my Body which will be given up for you" and then the priest purposefully pauses again when he holds up the chalice after saying "This is the chalice of my Blood…Do this in memory of me". These special pauses in the Eucharistic Prayer are designed to provide us with a few moments to stop and recognize how much we are loved by Jesus. These are moments for us to pause and reflect with wonder, awe, adoration, and thanksgiving as we marvel at Jesus' unwavering commitment to us and his promise of eternal friendship despite our obvious flaws and failings. In some churches, altar servers ring bells during this time of the Mass as a way of saying: "Pay attention! What just happened is a big deal! This is a special time to pray."

Indeed, this is an extraordinary opportunity to contemplate Jesus' great love *for* us.

ANAMNESIS

The Priest:
The mystery of faith.
The people:
We proclaim your Death, O Lord,
and profess your Resurrection
until you come again.
Or
When we eat this Bread and drink this Cup,
we proclaim your Death, O Lord,
until you come again.
Or
Save us, Savior of the world,
for by your Cross and Resurrection
you have set us free.

The Priest:
Eucharistic Prayer II:
Therefore, as we celebrate
the memorial of his Death and Resurrection…

Eucharistic Prayer III:
Therefore, O Lord, as we celebrate the memorial
of the saving Passion of your Son,
his wondrous Resurrection
and Ascension into heaven,
and as we look forward to his second coming…

This is a very different kind of mystery.
Throughout much of Christian history, Christians have called the celebration of the Mass the celebration of the "sacred myster-

ies". This terminology finds its way into many of the prayers we use in the Mass today. For example, after the words of consecration, the priest says: "The mystery of faith".

It is quite easy for us to interpret these words in the wrong way. For most of us, the first thing that comes to mind when we talk about mysteries are TV detective shows we binge watch or mystery novels that keep us up late at night until the mystery is solved and the case is closed. In these sorts of "mysteries", protagonists intentionally hide their actions until someone uncovers their secret.

The use of the word "mystery" during the Mass actually has a very different meaning. The word "mystery" in Catholic terminology is not about a reality that is intentionally hidden from us, but rather, a reality that has been revealed to us that is so profound, so meaningful, and so deep that there is always more about this reality that we can discover.

We will never fully comprehend or fully grasp with our minds the mystery of God's love because it is so much deeper and more intense than we could ever comprehend. Over time, our knowledge of God's love for us and God's plan of salvation grows, but there will always be more and more for us to learn. This is especially true at the Mass. As we enter into the Mass, there will always be new insights we can gain into God's love and his plan of salvation.

One key element of the Eucharistic Prayer is *anamnesis*. This Greek word means "remembering" and has its roots in the Jewish tradition of prayerfully remembering God's major interventions in the lives of his people. Jewish people would regularly recall these major events in their history through the celebration of feast days. *Anamnesis* helped the people to grow in their understanding of God's work. It was also a way for them to grow in their relationship with the God who had acted in the past and would continue to act in their lives. The people grew in their ability to have confidence in God's providence because of their sacred remembering.

During these celebrations, the people were not just nostalgically telling old stories, but they spiritually were entering into the reality, the mystery, that took place in those historic events. The people of Israel recognized that whenever God acts in history his eternal power and love are unleashed and cannot be contained in just one static moment of time. They understood that the same divine power and love was accessible to them in the present moment when they remembered God's actions from the past.

Jesus encouraged his disciples to continue this pattern of *anamnesis* on the night of the Last Supper, telling them: "Do this in remembrance of me". During the Eucharistic Prayer, the congregation heeds this request of Jesus by saying one of three different memorial acclamations, such as: "We proclaim your Death, O Lord, and profess your Resurrection until you come again".

As the Eucharistic Prayer continues, these acclamations are quickly followed by the priest praying an *anamnesis*, which highlights that the Mass is indeed the memorial of Jesus' death and resurrection.[28]

Again, these words are not just a sentimental remembering of ancient events. As we recall these sacred events from Jesus' life, we encounter the divine love expressed in those moments in the past.[29] For example, the merciful love that Jesus showed as he suffered and died on the cross is made present during the Eucharistic Prayer as we remember his suffering and death. The merciful love Jesus offered to the repentant criminal dying next to him on Calvary. The merciful love Jesus gave on Calvary to those cruel men who had tortured him and crucified him, as he prayed: "Father, forgive them, they know not what they do" (Luke 23:34). This same merciful love is made present to us during the *anamnesis*!

The peace that Jesus shared with his disciples on the day of his resurrection is also available to us, as we remember his resurrection during the Eucharistic Prayer. The Son of God, Jesus Christ, approaches us with the same reassurance he gave his fearful and anxious friends on the day of his resurrection saying: "Peace be with you" (Luke 24:36; John 20:19, 21). "Do not be afraid!" (Matthew 28:10).

As we recall Jesus' Ascension into heaven, he empowers us with the same grace he gave his disciples while commissioning them to continue his mission in the world. We receive strength to go out into the world and share our faith. Our hope is also strengthened, as we remember Jesus' parting promise that he would prepare a place for us in heaven (John 14:2).[30]

As we begin to appreciate the depth of God's saving plan that we encounter during the Mass, the natural response within our hearts is wonder and gratitude. Because of the beauty and depth of our encounter with the mystery of God during the Mass, an essential element of our participation in the Mass is reverence. The culture of the Mass is supposed to be very different than the culture of noise, distraction, busyness, and entertainment that surrounds us most other moments of our life. The Mass is purposefully carried out with a reverent pace that makes space for us to ponder, to reflect, and to contemplate the mystery of God's goodness towards us.

THE OBLATION

The Priest:
Eucharistic Prayer II:
...we offer you, Lord,
the Bread of life and the Chalice of salvation,
giving thanks that you have held us worthy
to be in your presence and minister to you.

Eucharistic Prayer III:
...we offer you in thanksgiving
this holy and living sacrifice.

Look, we pray, upon the oblation of your Church
and, recognizing the sacrificial Victim by whose death
you willed to reconcile us to yourself...

A Christian girl named Therese wanted to do something big for God. Therese had grown up in an upper middle-class family. Her mother owned a successful business. In her comfortable childhood, Therese saw firsthand the success of her hardworking and intelligent parents.

Like most young adults who grow up in such circumstances, Therese felt the need to be successful in her life too. She desired to do something to make a big impact on the world.

Therese was a deeply religious person and came up with the idea of becoming an international missionary. She was excited about travelling across the globe to serve people in need. Therese became more and more convinced that this would be how she could live a successful life and do something important for God. This was her dream for her future.

There was a problem however.

Actually, there were many problems.

The more Therese pursued her dream, the more the heart-breaking reality began to sink in that she did not have the ability to be a missionary.

Therese was very weak physically. She had major medical issues that sometimes left her bedridden for weeks. There was no way she could physically endure the challenges of international travel, a foreign diet, or a missionary lifestyle.

Therese was very weak emotionally as well. She had a streak of melancholy in her personality that became more pronounced as she dealt with the death of her mother from breast cancer. Therese struggled with deep sadness. She even struggled at certain moments of her life with thoughts of suicide.

Therese realized that she could not be anything she wanted to be. She would never become a missionary. Her dream to make a difference in the world would never come true. She would not be able to do the great things for God that she had imagined.

And this put her into a deep existential crisis. She began to freak out. She feared she would "miss out" on so much in life because of her physical and emotional struggles. How would her life be meaningful? How would she be able to do something for God? What would she have to look forward to each day when she woke up?

Reading the Bible one day, Therese came to St. Paul's words about love in the twelfth and thirteenth chapters of his First Letter to the Corinthians. St. Paul explains how God has given different roles to different people in the Body of Christ but these roles mean nothing if a person is not a person of love. St. Paul says choosing to love is the true measure of Christian greatness. Whether or not someone chooses to love is more important than whether or not someone is a prestigious teacher, leader, missionary, or martyr. Because love is the ultimate reason why we are here on earth.

These words helped Therese overcome her crisis and figure out her future. Because of her medical issues and emotional issues, her life would never be as glamorous as she had planned.

However, St. Paul's words helped her see that this was OK because her life could still have deep purpose and meaning if she chose to be a person of sincere love.

Therese began to live differently. She stopped hanging on so tightly to her own dreams, focusing instead on little acts of kindness. Eventually, she entered a cloistered community of religious sisters and dedicated herself to a lifestyle of humble love.

She approached her mundane chores in the convent as acts of love. They were simple acts like peeling potatoes, scrubbing floors, and dealing with the abrasive personalities of other sisters. Yet, Therese put all of her heart into these everyday tasks so that they would be acts of deep love.

Therese died young. She was only 24 years old. Yet, the Catholic Church eventually canonized her a saint and Pope John Paul II named her a Doctor of the Church.

The fact that Therese became a doctor of the Church is quite significant. This title is usually reserved for accomplished theologians, professors, and preachers. St. Therese is a doctor of the Church because she taught through her words and example that the ultimate purpose of life is love. Chasing after our dreams is actually not the most important thing in life. Accepting God's dream for us is what actually brings meaning to our lives.

God's dream for us is to live a life of love. The way we do something great for God is by offering ourselves in obedient service to his divine plan as we choose to love in the simple circumstances of daily life.

Time and time again in the Old Testament, the people of Israel tried to do something to please God. They attempted to do something sacrificial to show their allegiance to God. Oftentimes, this involved ritual sacrifice of animals or offering a portion of their harvest.[31] These sacrificial offerings were also called "oblations".

For example, the people would offer to God their best animal, an unblemished animal, demonstrating they were willing to sacrifice something precious to God.[32] Their sacrifice was an attempt to prove that their attachment to God was more important than their attachment to the material things that God had created like animals or produce from their fields.

These sacrifices were often offered to God through a ritual fire. A fire completely consuming the offering was a way of showing that their offering was a total gift to God and was for his benefit and his glory alone. A burnt offering of this kind was called a "holocaust".

As salvation history unfolded in the Old Testament, God helped the people understand that these sacrifices were not the perfect way to please God. Animal sacrifices were not the ultimate way God desired his people to show their love and allegiance to him. Rather, the people would prove their dedication by prayer and worship, following the commandments, and loving each other (Psalm 40:7-11; Isaiah 1:11-15; Amos 5:21-24; Micah 6; Proverbs 21:3).

The way people could do something "great" for God was by obediently following the commandments and living everyday life with great love for God and neighbor.

Oftentimes, the people struggled to fulfill this divine request. They instead found that offering animal sacrifices was much easier than dedicating their actions in daily life to God and allowing God to shape all of their priorities and decisions.

During the Eucharistic Prayer, the priest prays a special prayer of oblation. The oblation offered to God at the Mass is not an animal sacrifice or an offering of farm produce. Rather, it is the one, perfect fulfilment of what God had asked of humanity throughout salvation history. The oblation at Mass is the self-offering of Jesus who lived his daily life with total fidelity to God's commandments and lived his daily life with faithful, persevering love.[33] From the quiet moments of his life as a carpenter in an obscure town called Nazareth to the crucial moments of his public ministry in Jerusalem, Jesus lived life with total love and dedication to God. Jesus' loving obedience culminated in his journey to Calvary where he gave us the perfect example of total dedication to serving God and loving neighbor.

Jesus chose to love and to be faithful to God the Father even as he entered into the worst human experience possible - a situation of betrayal, excruciating physical suffering, terrible emotional pain, ruthless torture, spiritual agony, and physical death. Jesus was teaching us that even the most miserable of human experiences can be places where we do something beautiful for God whenever we choose to stay faithful to God's commandments and choose to love.

During the Eucharistic Prayer, we are incorporated into Jesus' loving oblation, his self-offering.[34] The priest prays that God the Father will accept the offering of our lives, incorporated through the Mass into Jesus' one, perfect sacrifice – his total offering of himself to the Father.

Certainly, our dedication, our faithfulness, and our love are lacking when compared to the total and unwavering way Jesus offered his life to the Father. Yet, Jesus in his mercy gives us the opportunity to be united with his perfect sacrifice, as he purifies us to become an offering that is deeply pleasing to God.

The oblation during the Eucharistic Prayer is a time to offer consciously to God the various aspects of our lives that we reflected upon during the Preparation of the Gifts. We unite ourselves to Jesus on the altar and gratefully acknowledge that the simple acts of our everyday life are united to his total self-offering. Yardwork, office work, laundry, cooking, cleaning, exercise, paying bills, all our daily tasks enter into the oblation of our lives at this moment of the Mass. This is why our daily routine takes on new, eternal meaning because of the Mass!

As St. Therese learned, to make a true oblation of our lives requires accepting that our life will not always look the way we had dreamed. This is true of our big dreams, such as our plans for marriage, family life, and a career. But it is also true for smaller plans as well. Offering to God the inconveniences of daily life is an essential part of what is happening at this moment in the Mass. The traffic jam on the way to work. The diaper change in the middle of dinner. The unexpected bill right before Christmas. We offer all of this to God. We offer our life as it is now and not some idealized version of it. During the

Mass, our real life is incorporated into Jesus' offering of love, his one perfect sacrifice to the Father. In this way, we enter into his obedient acceptance of the Father's plan for his life.

St. Therese had it right. What is most important is not how impressive, dramatic, or heroic our daily existence might appear. Our daily existence, even when humdrum and unexciting, can become something special. When we are consciously living our daily routine as a preparation for the Mass, even the humblest situations become places where we can do something meaningful for God.

THE SECOND EPICLESIS

Nobody likes taxes.

The first time I visited the Holy Land, our guide explained that the Roman government controlled the area where Jesus lived his adult life and carried out his ministry. The Roman government charged heavy taxes on items anyone would sell in that region. At tax collection posts along the roads, a Roman official, a publican, would stop those passing by and charge them significant taxes on the goods they were carrying.

The people hated paying these taxes and hated the publicans who enforced these taxes. They hated the tax collectors because they typically extorted them by charging higher rates than Rome required. The tax collectors used these extra profits to fund their comfortable, affluent lifestyles. The simple people often struggled to make ends meet and feed their families, while tax collectors lived the high life and partied hard with the money they had forced the people to pay in "taxes".

There was nothing the simple people could do to change the system. Everyone had been a victim of the greedy tax collectors. None of the hardworking people had any esteem for publicans.

Thus, it is no surprise that Jesus' choice to call Matthew, a tax collector, to be one of his close colleagues and disciples created a huge scandal among the people of that region. Then Jesus further shocked the people by visiting the home of Matthew and socializing with other tax collectors as they partied. The people were puzzled. Didn't Jesus know that they were a bunch of scumbags?

Jesus responded to their murmuring by saying: "Those who are well do not need a physician, but the sick do. Go and learn the meaning of the words, 'I desire mercy, not sacrifice'" (Matthew 9:12-13). The people must have been thinking: "But these tax collectors have taken so much from us! They should not be given a chance to be part of God's Kingdom."

Our tour guide in the Holy Land emphasized that a tax collector like Matthew would have been hated by everyone in the small towns where Jesus lived and carried out his ministry. Tax collectors like Matthew would have cheated everyone in these towns *including the other men whom Jesus chose to be his apostles.*

Imagine how fishermen like Peter, Andrew, James and John would have been filled with resentment when, after a long night on the sea, they begrudgingly had to hand over to Matthew a significant share of their profits from the fish they had worked so hard to catch and would sell to support their families.

How difficult it must have been for those early apostles to welcome and to accept Matthew into their core group of colleagues. What heroics acts of forgiveness it must have taken for these fishermen to share meals with Matthew and to sit next to him as Jesus taught and mentored them as a group.

It is important to realize that there were times when tension, misunderstanding, hurt, resentment, and frustration existed between the first followers of Jesus. Jesus was not speaking about abstract or hypothetical situations when he taught frequently about humility, patience, forgiveness, reconciliation, and peace. He was speaking about the relationships that existed between his disciples and their struggles to love and to forgive each other.

Jesus spent a significant amount of time during his earthly life teaching his disciples how to forgive each other and grow in unity. In fact, on the night of the Last Supper, Jesus prayed for unity among his disciples asking that their relationships might reflect the unity that exists between God the Father and God the Son through the Holy Spirit (John 17:11).

During the Eucharistic Prayer, there is a second *epiclesis* ("calling down") prayer asking that Jesus' prayer for unity among his disciples might be realized in us through our participation in the Mass. Through our reception of Holy Communion, the same Jesus who worked tirelessly to bring about unity among his disciples is at work in our midst helping us to forgive, to show compassion to each other, and to grow in unity. This portion of the Eucharistic Prayer asks for an outpouring of the Holy Spirit upon us so that the power of the Holy Spirit who unites God the Father and God the Son might unite us closer to each other through participation in the Mass.

The Holy Spirit has been working to bring unity among members of the Church from the first days of Christianity after Jesus ascended into heaven. A clear example of the fruit of the Holy Spirit's unifying work in the early Church is St. Paul. Saul was a zealous anti-Christian fanatic who had gone to great lengths to terrorize and murder Christians. After Saul went through a dramatic conversion, the Christian community not only welcomed him, but also helped him become a leader in the Church.

Can you imagine what heroic acts of forgiveness the early Christians must have made to welcome into their community someone like Paul who had been killing fellow parishioners, clergy, friends, and family members?

The Christian community from its earliest beginnings has been a community of forgiveness and mercy. The same divine power that empowered the early Christians to forgive heroically is accessible to us through our participation in the Mass.

Forgiveness is both a choice and a process.

It begins with recognizing the wrong that someone has done to us. Forgiveness does not mean ignoring hurtful actions or justifying what others have wrongly done to us. When we forgive someone, we acknowledge the full reality of how someone has hurt us, but we decide to love that person anyway.

Forgiveness is a choice to participate in Jesus' loving mercy towards sinners, as we choose to love them despite the wrong they have done. When we forgive, we are choosing not to define other people only by their faults. We are choosing to see sinners with the perspective of God who sees their goodness and potential, as well as their obvious brokenness and sinfulness.

Forgiveness is a choice to love another person. It is decision to will their good and to want what is best for them. A sign that we have forgiven someone is if we are able to pray for the good of the person who has hurt us. A sign we have not fully forgiven someone is if we wish harm upon that person or if we actively seek ways to bring unnecessary pain and hardship into their life.

Forgiveness is not primarily a feeling. Even after forgiving someone, there still might be moments when feelings of anger, sadness, or hurt fill our hearts as we remember the wrong done to us. In these moments, we need to go through the process again of making the choice to forgive the person, pray for their good, and acknowledge that these negative feelings towards this person might actually be a healthy emotional reaction to the wrong this person has committed against us.

I can't help but wonder if Simon Peter had Matthew the tax collector in mind when he asked Jesus how often he must forgive a brother who offends him (Matthew 18:21-22)?

Jesus' response to this question was that there must be no limits to the forgiveness Christians offer to people who hurt them. Jesus challenged Simon Peter to believe that he could live a lifestyle of forgiveness that would reflect God's patient mercy. Jesus challenged Simon Peter to believe that he could bring peace to Simon Peter's heart that had been hurt and wounded by the offenses of people like Matthew the tax collector.

During this section of the Eucharistic Prayer, we are asking the Holy Spirit to help us forgive each other and grow in unity as members of the Body of Christ. We are praying that we might follow the example of Simon Peter and the other apostles who forgave people like Matthew the tax collector. Some of the people in the pews with us at Mass have offended us. A complaining family member. A rude parent at the parish school. An arrogant parish staff member. Despite these typical tensions, the power of this *epiclesis* during the Eucharistic Prayer and reception of Holy Communion make it possible for us to forgive and grow closer together, as members of the Body of Christ. This is a time during Mass to invite the Holy Spirit to work within our relationships, especially within our church family.

THE INTERCESSIONS: OUR POPE, OUR BISHOP, AND THE CLERGY

The Priest:
Eucharistic Prayer II:
Remember, Lord, your Church,
spread throughout the world,
and bring her to the fullness of charity,
together with N. our Pope and N. our Bishop
and all the clergy.

Eucharistic Prayer III:
May this sacrifice of our reconciliation,
we pray, O Lord,
advance the peace and salvation of all the world.
Be pleased to confirm in faith and charity
your pilgrim Church on earth,
with your servant N. our Pope and N. our Bishop,
the Order of Bishops, all the clergy,
and the entire people you have gained for your own.

I always marveled at how far he had come to get there.

Four of the five years I studied in Rome, I lived in a room with spectacular views of St. Peter's Basilica. As I sat at my desk studying for my graduate degree, my eyes and mind would often wander out the window towards the majestic church built over the tomb of St. Peter.

I always found myself amazed at how far he had come to get there.

Simon Peter ended up a long way from the quiet scenery of the Sea of Galilee that he called home. The humble fisherman left the small town he had known his whole life and travelled to the capital city of the Roman Empire. In Rome, the "retired" fisherman probably had to use an interpreter when he spoke, since he likely did not know the sophisticated language of the capital. In fact, many theorize that Simon Peter was illiterate.

To make a modern-day comparison, Simon Peter's journey to become a leader of the Church in Rome would be something like an uneducated farmer from Africa becoming one of the most important religious figures in Washington DC or in New York City.

If Simon Peter had chosen for his life to unfold according to his own plan, he would have spent his entire life on a quiet lake in the Middle East. Instead, he accepted God's plan, which took him to the bustling, sophisticated, and crowded capital of the Roman Empire. Simon Peter had left behind the family fishing business that had been his livelihood. He had left behind the beautiful lake and the camaraderie of his friends in his village. Walking away from the place and lifestyle most familiar to him, Simon Peter accepted the adventure Jesus had prepared for him: to preach the Gospel in Rome.

Simon Peter said "yes" to Jesus' call to serve the Church to point of eventually dying as a martyr. The place where he died in Rome is now where the magnificent Basilica of St. Peter stands in his memory.

During the Eucharist Prayer, the successor to St. Peter, the bishop of Rome, is remembered by name. This is a moment during the Mass when we pray for the man, commonly referred to as the pope, who Jesus has called, like St. Peter, to give up his own plans for his life and to serve the Church in a special role of leadership. We also recognize the local bishop by name during the

Eucharistic Prayer. We pray for his ministry and the ministry of all priests.

The reason we acknowledge the pope and the local bishop during the Mass is theologically very significant.[35] The ministry of these men ties us to the Last Supper when Jesus instituted the Eucharist and gave the first apostles the command: "Do this in remembrance of me" (1 Corinthians 11:24-25). These apostles eventually appointed successors to continue their apostolic ministry by laying hands on them. Today this tradition of unbroken succession endures as bishops solemnly lay hands on the heads of men in ordination rites to appoint them as priests or bishops.

The men God has chosen to serve as leaders in the Church are not perfect. Simon Peter himself denied his relationship with Jesus not just once, but three times during Jesus' Passion. Of course, Jesus also chose Judas Iscariot to be a leader in the Christian community. Judas ended up betraying Jesus and then taking his own life.

Similar to Jesus' first apostles, the leaders of the Church today are weak, human instruments who have their own struggles with sin. However, our belief is that Jesus uses these weak, sinful men to continue his ministry and works through their words and actions in the sacraments of the Church. For this reason, it is laudable to have a healthy respect for clergy and to be grateful for the sacrifices they make to serve the Church.

At the same time, it is important not to put clergy on a pedestal that precludes them from being accountable for their actions or their sinfulness. In fact, during the Eucharistic Prayer the Institution Narrative often begins with the words "on the night he [Jesus] was betrayed". These words recall Judas' betrayal of Jesus and stand as a perennial reminder that clergy sometimes will fail. These words broadcasting the weakness of one of the chosen apostles clearly indicate that covering up the sinfulness of clergy is never a truly Christian approach. The Church perpetually points out during the Mass the betrayal of Judas, reinforcing the need for us to put our faith ultimately in Jesus. We place our faith not in the clergy, but rather in Jesus who is working through his clergy in the sacraments.

During this time of the Mass, we pray that all clergy in the Church will grow in virtue and persevere in the call they have received. We give thanks for their ministry, which connects us to the first apostles gathered in the Upper Room on the night when Jesus was betrayed. We pray that like Simon Peter they will allow Jesus to lead them beyond their own plans and preferences, giving of themselves wholeheartedly to serve the Church no matter what it might cost them. This is also an appropriate time in the Mass to pray for all the young men who Jesus is calling to begin the path of preparation for the priesthood. Jesus is asking them to let go of their own plans and the limits set by their own selfishness. He is asking them, like Simon Peter, to offer their lives in service to the Church.

THE INTERCESSIONS: COMMEMORATION OF THE DEAD

The Priest:
Eucharistic Prayer II:
Remember also our brothers and sisters
who have fallen asleep in the hope of the resurrection,
and all who have died in your mercy:
welcome them into the light of your face.

Eucharistic Prayer III:
To our departed brothers and sisters
and to all who were pleasing to you
at their passing from this life,
give kind admittance to your kingdom.
There we hope to enjoy the fullness of your glory
through Christ our Lord,
through whom you bestow on the world all that is good.

Back in the 1960s, Dr. Elisabeth Kübler-Ross was trying to do research in a Chicago area hospital. Dr. Kübler-Ross wanted to interview patients who were terminally ill or in the final stages of their lives. She became frustrated very quickly because no one seemed to want to help her. No one wanted to talk about death.

This was at a time well before hospice care and palliative care were commonplace in hospitals. Dr. Kübler-Ross shared in one of her books[36] how she kept asking other physicians: "Where are the patients who are dying? Where are the patients who are nearing death? I would like to talk to them." The answer she received was often the same: "We do not have any of those kind of people in this hospital."

This response frustrated her. She knew from hospital records that people died there every day. Quickly she recognized that she had already gained a crucial insight for her research.

She realized that the culture was in denial about death.

While physicians claimed no patients were dying or nearing death, the truth was that each day every single person in the hospital was nearer to the moment of their death than the previous day. All of us draw closer to death every single moment of our lives.

Most people in the Western world today do not like talking about death or getting too close to it.

And yet, if we look at the life of Jesus, we see a very different attitude towards death. Jesus confronted the reality of death in all its sadness and horror! This is true of his own death, but also of the deaths of others.

Think, for example, of when Jesus visited the tomb of his friend Lazarus and cried because of his death (John 11:35).

Or consider Luke 7:11-17 when Jesus approached the dead body of a man in the city of Nain. Jesus had just worked an amazing miracle, healing a very ill man in a nearby town. We can imagine the joy and excitement of the large crowd travelling with Jesus. It was a really good day for them, until they encountered a tragically sad scene.

A large crowd of people was leaving through the narrow gate of a town. A funeral procession. As Jesus and the people with him drew closer, they began to learn details about the man's death. He was an only son. His father was already dead. His poor mother was now a widow.

With our modern attitude towards death, we would be tempted when confronted by such a scene to back away to allow the sorrow and tragedy pass by at a distance. Then we could continue on, as unaffected as possible, on our merry way. We would try to insulate ourselves from the heart-wrenching sadness of death.

Yet, Jesus could not stay away from such a painful situation. He entered into this scene of death and grief. Then he did something that would have shocked his followers. Jesus touched death! Jesus touched the coffin of the dead man!

Touching death made a person ritually "unclean" in Jesus' time. A person generally did not want to get that close to death unless absolutely necessary. Jesus did not care. He reached out and entered into the scene of mourning. Jesus refused to distance himself from death.

In fact, Jesus not only physically touched death in touching the coffin, but he allowed the suffering of the grieving mother to touch him as well. The gospel of Luke said: "When the Lord saw her, he was moved with pity for her" (7:13). The phrase in the original Greek text indicates that Jesus was "deeply shaken up" and "touched to the core of his being" by the sadness of the mother. He did not run away from the depressing scene, but chose to be present as a source of compassion and hope.

Throughout the gospel of Luke, Jesus faced death head-on. In Luke 9:51, Jesus turned his face towards Jerusalem to face his own suffering and death. After his arrival in Jerusalem, Jesus experienced his agony in the garden, confronting the horror of his own death with an attitude of trusting acceptance and hope.

Jesus did not shy away from death because he wanted us to be able to face our own death with the same attitude of hope and trust in God's care for us. Jesus refused to be in denial of death and to stay away from it because his mission was to lead us through the tragedy of death to the glory of life with God forever in heaven.

In the Eucharistic Prayer, we always remember persons who have died. While this remembrance might bring sadness to our hearts, the presence of the risen Jesus in our midst in the Eucharist gives us hope that those who have died are now living a new life with God in heaven. The prayers of the Catholic Funeral Mass remind us that for our beloved dead, "life is changed, not ended" and our relationship with those who have died continues after death.[37]

The prayers we offer during Mass for the deceased are acts of love. God generously chooses to use our prayerful acts of love to help our deceased loved ones experience his merciful love that brings eternal salvation. Through the Mass, Jesus sustains our relationships with the dead as he draws us more deeply into communion with each other.

The *Catechism of the Catholic Church* puts it this way:

> In the Eucharist, the Church expresses her efficacious communion with the departed: offering to the Father in the Holy Spirit the sacrifice of the death and resurrection of Christ, she asks to purify his child of his sins and their consequences, and to admit him to the Paschal fullness of the table of the Kingdom. It is by the Eucharist thus celebrated that the community of the faithful, especially the family of the deceased, learn to live in communion with the one who "has fallen asleep in the Lord," by communicating in the Body of Christ of which he is a living member and, then, by praying for him and with him.[38]

At the Mass, our relationship with people who have died continues in Christ who is uniting us closer together as brothers and sisters, members of his one Body. Jesus is working through our prayers for people who have died and through the prayers our deceased offer for us, as he opens us to a greater appreciation of our relationships with each other that, through him, can live on into eternity.

For many centuries, a common practice in the Church has been to schedule the remembrance of a specific person as the priest's primary intention for the celebration of each Mass. This custom reminds everyone at the Mass to pray for their relatives, friends, and all the deceased during the Eucharistic Prayer. This is an opportunity to pray for our deceased grandpa, cousin, sister, classmate, or neighbor – whoever has died in our family and community. We also pray for the deceased who have no one to pray for them.

The prayers we offer for the dead during the Eucharistic Prayer also prepare us for our own death. These prayers push us to accept the constant "letting go" that is necessary in earthly life. Throughout our lives, we have many moments when we must let go of certain dreams for the future and experience a "mini-death", a taste of death. In this way, we are constantly dying. Many of our plans for the future never come true. We lose what is precious to us. The circumstances of life as we prefer do not last. Our perceived control over our life circumstances is fleeting, temporary, and unsustainable.

While all of this sounds terribly depressing to our modern ears, Jesus reassures us that we do not need to be afraid. We do not need to panic. We do not need to let a dark cloud of gloom weigh us down. We are not only constantly dying, but we are also constantly rising. Jesus is with us in the Mass, and he is leading us deeper into his death *and* resurrection. He is leading us through death with an attitude of hope and trust that will lead us to the joy of the resurrection.

Jesus has made death into a place where his love is revealed and released into the world. At Mass, we experience this love and it creates deeper bonds of communion and connection between us that will live beyond our earthly graves.

At every Mass, we actually *celebrate* Jesus' death because it fills us with confidence and hope to face death in our own lives. Jesus has transformed death into a pathway to new life. Because of Jesus, our dying *always* leads to new life.

THE INTERCESSIONS: MARY, JOSEPH, AND ALL THE SAINTS

The Priest:
Eucharistic Prayer II:
Have mercy on us all, we pray,
that with the Blessed Virgin Mary, Mother of God,
with blessed Joseph, her Spouse,
with the blessed Apostles,
and all the Saints who have pleased you throughout
   the ages,
we may merit to be coheirs to eternal life,
and may praise and glorify you
through your Son, Jesus Christ.

Eucharistic Prayer III:
May he make of us
an eternal offering to you,
so that we may obtain an inheritance with your elect,
especially with the most Blessed Virgin Mary, Mother
   of God,
with blessed Joseph, her Spouse,
with your blessed Apostles and glorious Martyrs
(with Saint N.: the Saint of the day or Patron Saint)
and with all the Saints,
on whose constant intercession in your presence
we rely for unfailing help.

On one hand, this family was a very, very special family.

At every Mass the Eucharistic Prayer always mentions two saints in particular: Mary and Joseph.

Both saints had a very special role in God's plan of salvation, and the child they raised was the only Son of God. The Holy Family was certainly not a normal family. It was a very holy family.

At the same time, it would be a mistake to think that there are no similarities between the Holy Family and our own families. The humanity of the Holy Family should not be forgotten!

The Bible does not tell us much about the life of the Holy Family during Jesus' childhood at home in Nazareth. Those years probably were rather ordinary, filled with the typical tasks of a family routine at that time in history. There was likely not much to write about. For Joseph and Mary, these years would have included the "daily grind" of work and of parenting Jesus as he grew in wisdom and age into an adult (see Luke 2:52). These years would have been filled with the normal stuff of everyday family life: eating, socializing, prayer, work, household chores, and pretty much all the other human dealings that make up our own family lives.[39]

The handful of Biblical accounts we have on the life of the Holy Family are not stories of picture-perfect, Instagram-ready family life. In fact, most contain drama, tension, and challenges.

Take for example, the circumstances of Jesus' birth. Joseph and the very pregnant Mary had to make a several days journey on foot to a city that was a long distance from home (Luke 2:1-20). When they arrived in Bethlehem, the couple had to settle for sleeping in a stable for farm animals, since the city was already so packed full with visitors. Talk about a less than ideal place for a young pregnant woman to attempt to sleep! And then, to make matters worse, while in this stable, the time came for Mary to give birth to Jesus. This primitive setting was certainly not the type of place these parents had hoped would serve as the first nursery for their baby.

Then an unstable and ruthless dictator began persecuting

children out of fear of losing his throne to one of these innocent babies (Matthew 2:13-23). Joseph and Mary had to flee as refugees to Egypt, which took them even further from their home in Nazareth. They lived there for a significant period of time before finally making the long journey home with their young child.

After these stories, the Bible only tells us one more anecdote involving all three members of the Holy Family. This too was a situation of crisis in the life of the Holy Family (Luke 2:41-52). It was another period of great anxiety, misunderstanding, confusion, when things did not go the way these good parents had planned.

The event took place when Jesus was 12 years old. After the Holy Family celebrated the Passover together in Jerusalem, Joseph and Mary began their return trip home. However, because of a misunderstanding between them, they accidentally left Jesus behind on his own in Jerusalem. He was not part of the large group they were travelling with back to Nazareth.

Joseph and Mary began frantically searching for Jesus. But they did not find him.

They continued searching for him the next day as their anxiety levels continued to rise. But they did not find him.

Finally, after three days they found Jesus.

His distressed mother asked: "Son, why have you done this to us? Your father and I have been looking for you with great anxiety".

Jesus calmly dismissed his anxious parents' grave concern, responding: "Did you not know that I must be in my Father's house?"

Joseph and Mary "did not understand what he said to them" (Luke 2:48-50).

This incident should be reassuring to all of us who do not always understand our family members. Joseph and Mary may not have always understood Jesus' words and actions, let alone what was going on inside his mind and heart.

The remembrance of the Holy Family during the Eucharist Prayer reassures us that even though things in our families do not always go smoothly, our families can still be holy. The lives of Jesus, Mary, and Joseph teach us that a life of holiness is possible in the midst of normal, everyday family life. The lives of Jesus, Mary, and Joseph show us that moments of anxiety, misunderstanding, and frustration are actually moments when our families can become holy.

In challenging times, family members can either grow closer or farther apart. When we remember Mary and Joseph during the Eucharistic Prayer, we pray for God to help our family members grow closer to each other and closer to God through the challenges we face together. We are praying that we might fulfill the goal of family life and help our family members get to heaven.

Within our remembrance of the saints in the Eucharistic Prayer is an incredibly important petition. We ask God the Father to make it possible for us to become saints! We ask God in his mercy to grant us the gift of eternal salvation.

This is an important petition to make our own during the Eucharistic Prayer. We cannot merit heaven by our own powers or actions alone. Yet, God in his abundant generosity has opened to us the possibility of spending eternity in heaven. The remembrance of the saints during the Eucharistic Prayer should be comforting to us since they, like us, also struggled with human frailty, sinful habits, and innumerable difficulties. God's grace ultimately triumphed in the end, and made it possible for them to share in eternal glory. During the Eucharistic Prayer, we are praying that this same triumph will take place within us!

THE DOXOLOGY

The Priest:
Through him, and with him, and in him,
O God, almighty Father,
in the unity of the Holy Spirit,
all glory and honor is yours,
for ever and ever.
The People:
Amen.

Their friendship lasted 70 years.

I was lucky enough to grow up just a short distance from my grandparents. My family would visit them frequently, especially on Sunday afternoons when I was a child. When I eventually moved away from my home town, I still tried to visit them regularly.

My grandmother would spend several minutes of my visits giving what I describe as a "political lecture" to me and anyone else who was visiting at the time. My grandmother felt very strongly that only one particular American political party had the candidates who best promoted Catholic social teaching and the authentic good of our country. In her monologues, grandma would repeat over and over how she did not understand how any good Catholic or any deeply intelligent person would vote for a candidate from the other major political party.

Around the year 2011, those lectures ended. Grandma rarely talked about politics anymore when I visited.

And then it began to make sense.

My grandmother stopped lecturing on politics about the same time my grandfather passed away. I realized that those political lectures over the years were not intended so much for me, but rather, for my grandfather - a faithful member of the opposite political party.

I am pretty sure she knew my grandfather would sit politely and listen when grandkids were present, so she took advantage of the situation whenever we visited to say something to attempt to sway his political views to the other side of the political fence.

She was not very successful.

And this is precisely why I marvel at the deep friendship of my grandparents and look up to them as models of Christian marriage.

My grandma and grandpa were married for almost 70 years to someone whom they did not always agree with. That was obvious to all of us who knew them. Yet, never once did I ever have doubts about whether they loved each other. Their strong bond of love was just as apparent as the obvious differences in their opinions, personalities, and preferences.

What united them in love so strongly? What bonded them even though there were plenty of reasons they could have gone in opposite directions?

Growing up in a world where commitment and lasting friendships of any kind seem practically nonexistent, most members of my generation – the millennials – have often wondered whether it is worth investing in deep relationships. We have felt the pain of divorce first hand in the relationships of our own parents or in our own marriages. We have also been disappointed by the breakdown of our friendships with siblings, close peers, work colleagues, or childhood friends. Sometimes it can feel like growing close and staying close to other people is impossible in the cut-throat, fast-paced lifestyle today's culture urges us to live.

Is faithfulness to commitment possible today?

And if it is possible, is it really worth the effort and the sacrifice?

We find the answer to these questions in the fundamental

storyline that undergirds all of salvation history in the Bible.

The Old Testament emphasized how God desired to form a deep, lasting, and intimate bond with his people. This bond was called a covenant. God promised that he would always be committed to his people and love them faithfully. The people were to reciprocate this commitment and love God faithfully as well. Knowing that the people would be tempted to be unfaithful, God promised to help them grow closer together as a community. They would not just have their own individual relationships with God, but they would be able to rely on each other for support and encouragement when they were tempted to be unfaithful to God. Their covenant with God committed them to growing in mutual love with each other as well.

The Old Testament contains stories of elaborate rituals the people performed to show that they were serious about being faithful to their special relationship with God. These elaborate rituals often involved sprinkling of animal blood or animal sacrifices, which seem rather bizarre to our modern Western sensibilities.

However, we have to remember that at this time in history these people hunted and butchered animals to eat on a daily basis. To them, performing a ritual with animal blood was not gross at all. The sprinkling of blood symbolized that they would rather die than ruin their special relationship with God. They were promising to cooperate with what God wanted, which was a friendship that would include mutual faithfulness and dedication.

We know what happened don't we?

The people broke their promise to God.

In fact, many times in the Old Testament, the people were not able to stay faithful to their commitment to God. The people ruined their relationship with God and with each other. They chose to go in a different direction than what they had promised during the sacred ceremonies. They "hardened their hearts" and stubbornly refused God's help to become a true community.

Thankfully, the Holy Trinity had a solution to the people's

unfaithfulness to their promises. The Son of God took on flesh and entered into our weak human state. The Son of God entered into our humanity so that he, as a member of the human family, might make it possible for us to choose in a definitive way to be faithful to a covenant relationship with God the Father and to form true community with each other.

Jesus' whole life was a faithful "yes" to a covenant relationship of love. Jesus lived his human life with total faithfulness to God the Father. Jesus dedicated himself unselfishly to serving other people and forming true community with them. Jesus fulfilled God's original plan for humanity!

At every Mass, we have a chance to enter into the "yes" to the covenant lifestyle of love that Jesus lived throughout his entire life here on earth. Jesus knows we are weak and knows we are sinners. Jesus knows we are not always inclined to be faithful. Jesus knows we are tempted to stray from our commitments. And so, Jesus gave us the Mass as a way to enter into his choice to be faithful to the covenant of love that God the Father offers to us.

In fact, at the end of the Eucharistic Prayer we enter into Jesus' "yes" to a lifestyle of covenant love by saying "Amen!", which means: "so be it!" Through Jesus, with Jesus, and in Jesus, we commit ourselves to the lifestyle of unselfish love that gives glory and honor to God our Father. Through Jesus, with him, and in him, we make an offering of ourselves to God the Father as we say "Amen". Through him, with him, and in him we are able to make the choice to stay faithful to God and to our commitments to other people.

During the great "Amen" at the end of the Eucharistic Prayer, we accept Jesus' affirmative answer to the question: "Is faithfulness to commitment possible today?"

During the great "Amen" at the end of the Eucharistic Prayer, we accept Jesus' affirmative answer to the question: "Is faithfulness to commitment really worth all the effort and sacrifice?"

We join our voice to Jesus' "yes" to a lifestyle of loving commitment as we say "Amen".

As Mass continues, our reception of Jesus' Body and Blood lifts us up into the unbreakable bond of love that Jesus shares with God the Father and his people. In this way, reception of Holy Communion gives us strength to be true to the commitments we have made in our own lives. Holy Communion makes it possible for us to embrace true community and to live unselfishly.

Some days when we arrive at Mass, we are struggling to love other people or struggling to keep God as the first priority in our lives. Thus, Jesus invites us during every Mass to enter into his faithful "Amen", to strengthen and bolster our commitment to what really matters most. Entering into Jesus' definitive and faithful "yes" fortifies our drifting, wavering hearts and directs us back into a lifestyle of loving faithfulness.

As I look back at my grandparents' marriage, I realize that there was a deep connection between the Mass and their friend-ship. They attended Mass together not only every Sunday, but on most weekdays as well. The Eucharist provided them strength to love each other. It helped them remember the big picture and keep their arguments in perspective. Jesus helped them to be true to their commitment to love, even when they did not agree with each other!

THE COMMUNION RITE

THE LORD'S PRAYER: OUR FATHER...

The Priest:
At the Savior's command
and formed by divine teaching,
we dare to say:
All:
Our Father, who art in heaven,
hallowed be thy name;

He was now an orphan.

Charles said the night his father died was the most alone he felt in his entire life.

His mother had passed away when Charles was just 8 years old. And he lost his only brother at 12. And now as a 20-year-old, Charles learned the terrible news that his father was gone.

His father had always been his "rock", a military veteran who everyone in town called "the Captain". He was a source of strength, encouragement, and stability for his son in tough times. The man of deep faith had taught his son the importance of both discipline and compassion.

The death of his father left Charles deeply unsettled and feeling completely alone.

Charles would later talk about how this shaped his spiritual life. The helplessness he felt as an orphan at age 20 actually pushed him deeper in his relationship with God.

In the months that followed, came a life-changing realization. Charles recognized that his father had been preparing him for his death for a long time. He had passed on a deep faith to his son, readying him for the day when he would no longer be physically present and Charles would need to rely on God to be his "rock".

Charles understood that the love, strength, and support his father had given to him were all a reflection of God's fatherly love for him. The confidence he had received during his life from the loving presence of his father was actually foreshadowing the deep confidence he could experience from his relationship with God the Father.

Over time, Charles began to experience the truth of the words in the First Letter of St. John: "See what love the Father has bestowed on us that we may be called children of God. Yet so we are!" (1 John 3:1)

All of us have moments in our lives when we feel like orphans. A parent or important mentor dies. A close family member with dementia no longer recognizes us. A parent moves away after a divorce.

Other "orphan moments" are subtler. We lose confidence after being berated by a boss, coach, or mentor who usually defends us. We feel abandoned after a friend gossips behind our back and betrays us. Loneliness grows as a spouse claims to be too busy for a deep conversation. We feel left behind when we do not receive an invitation to a social gathering.

All of us have had "orphan moments" when we felt alone, unsupported, and fearful about the future. We felt like orphans who have to fend for themselves with no one to support them.

In fact, this insecurity can be frequent because the world around us can be very harsh, uncaring, and unkind.

The words of the Our Father we pray at every Mass encourage us in these "orphan moments" to remember our identity as God's children. We have a Rock whose presence in our lives can bring confidence and strength when we feel alone and insecure. God is our Father who is with us and desires to support us when we are afraid and fearful about the future.

When we enter the church building for Mass, the typical custom is to dip our hand in holy water and make the Sign of the Cross to recall our Baptism. Baptism is when God claimed us as his beloved sons and daughters and promised us that his fatherly love would accompany us throughout the entirety of our lives. Every time we pray the Our Father, we are confessing our trust and confidence in God's fatherly love.

For Charles, his experiences of family love, the tragic death of his own father, and his experience of God's fatherly love paved the way for him to realize that his vocation was to reflect God's fatherly love to other people as a priest. Father Charles eventually became a bishop, cardinal, and then on October 16, 1978 Charles ("Karol" in Polish) Wojtyla became the pope: Pope John Paul II.[40]

One of the main messages Pope John Paul II preached over and over as holy father were words Jesus also repeated frequently: "Do not be afraid!" Pope John Paul II had learned from his own experience as an orphan that he did not need to be afraid and fearful about his future. Pope John Paul II wanted to share with people the secret to achieving the confidence he experienced when he allowed God the Father to be the Rock of stability and strength in his own life.

Praying the Our Father during the Mass, we acknowledge that God our Father in heaven is our Rock who has our back, who loves us, and desires to spend eternity with us in heaven.

The words of the Our Father are very familiar. Because these words are so commonplace, it might seem strange that the priest introduces the Lord's Prayer at Mass by saying: "At the Savior's command and formed by divine teaching we *dare* to say..."

Those words of introduction seem straight out of the mouths of children daring a friend to do something scary: "I *dare* you to do it! Actually, I *double-dare* you!"

What is so daring about saying a prayer that Christians often begin praying when they are little kids?

Actually, a lot. The Our Father prayer is much bolder than we realize.

To call God our Father is to assert that the all-powerful, all-knowing, all-holy, eternal, perfect, God desires deep intimacy with us who are fragile, weak, human, limited, contingent, and imperfect sinners.

To say that we have a place at the table with the three divine persons who are the God of the universe is an assertion that we would not dare to make up on our own - unless a trustworthy source told us that this is the truth.

Jesus taught us to call God our Father. He taught us to call God *Abba*, an affectionate term for a father, something similar to the terms "papa" or "daddy". Jesus taught that we can share in the closeness he enjoys with God the Father. This also means we can call Jesus our brother!

Praying the words of the Our Father is bold for another reason as well.

If we call God *our* Father, we are acknowledging that other people are God's children. They are also our brothers and sisters. We are part of a community, a large family, as we strive to live the Christian life. Being part of this community includes obligations and responsibilities that give us opportunities to reflect the unity of the Trinity in our relationships here on earth. We reflect the close relationships of the three persons of the Trinity when we treat others with love as our brothers and sisters, rather than as competitors, enemies, or rivals.

Implied in our praying of the Our Father is our commitment to building Christian community. The lack of vibrant Catholic community at a particular parish or in our region can be disheartening, but by praying the Lord's Prayer we are agreeing not to give up on our Father's design for a Kingdom of persons united in sincere relationships. We must dare to seek every opportunity possible to form strong bonds of connection with other Christians, as brothers and sisters of the same Father. Because of the isolation and individualism rampant in our times, it is essential for every Catholic to be proactive in building community. Never underestimate the long-term good that can result from introducing yourself to someone after Mass, inviting a Catholic neighbor to a social event, or joining a parish organization. Community is formed through one encounter, one conversation, or one prayer at a time.

The words of the Lord's Prayer are deeply sacred because they are the words of the Lord Jesus himself. He taught his disciples to pray using these words after they had seen him praying to God the Father and asked him for guidance in their own prayer (Luke 11:1-4).

St. Cyprian, writing in the middle of the third century, summarized well how we use Jesus' words to enter into his conversation with God the Father through the Lord's Prayer:

> So, my brothers, let us pray as God our master has taught us. To ask the Father in words his Son has given us, to let him hear the prayer of Christ ringing in his ears, is to make our prayer one of friendship, a family prayer. Let the Father recognize the words of his Son. Let the Son who lives in our hearts be also on our lips. We have him as an advocate for sinners before the Father; when we ask forgiveness for our sins, let us use the words given by our advocate. He tells us: "Whatever you ask the Father in my name, he will give you." What more effective prayer could we then make in the name of Christ than in the words of his own prayer?[41]

Using the words of Christ at this point of the Mass is deeply significant, since the Lord's Prayer begins the Rite of Communion. In the Eucharistic Prayer, Jesus welcomed us into his dialogue with the Father. This dialogue led us to offer our lives with Jesus to the Father, a commitment verbally expressed in our "Amen" to the Eucharistic Prayer. We dare to continue this dialogue through the Lord's Prayer, asking for "our daily bread". This petition is answered in Holy Communion.

THE LORD'S PRAYER: THY KINGDOM COME...

thy Kingdom come,
thy will be done
on earth as it is in heaven.

They were eight words that changed my life.

At a certain point in my life as a college student, I began to seriously consider priesthood. However, I was quickly overwhelmed by thinking about the sacrifices such a life entails.

Priesthood would mean giving up my plans for the future, especially for a career, wife, and family. At that time, the thought of going to seminary and becoming a priest made me feel like I had to give up *everything* that would bring me joy and fulfillment in my life.

Yet, deep down inside my heart was a sense that I needed to be open to the possibility of becoming a priest.

During that difficult time, a priest suggested I pray a simple prayer of eight words. These eight words changed my approach to everything.

"Lord, help me to want what you want."

Over time, this prayer began to work. I became more willing to let go of my own plans. More willing to face my fears. More willing to try to understand what God had planned for my life. I grew more willing to trust God with my life, not trying to control everything according to my own selfish desires.

It took plenty of time, but eventually I could say the words of the Our Father and actually mean all of them, including the phrase: "Thy Kingdom come, thy will be done, on earth as it is in heaven". I could pray for God's plan to be realized for my life, and more importantly, admit that God's plan for my future was better than my own.

God has a plan for our lives.

What is this plan?

Obviously, the concrete details for everyone are different, but the basics are really the same for all of us.

God wants us to experience love and to be able to show true love to others.

God wants us to experience true community and peace.

God wants us to be forgiven and to forgive others.

God wants us to experience endless joy one day in heaven.

God's plan is truly better than our plan. And yet, giving up what is familiar and comfortable to us can be quite difficult.

We often hang on tightly to the broken pieces of our lives – even though the only possible way for them to be put together into something beautiful (like a mosaic) is by the work of an all-knowing, all-powerful, and all-loving God.

In my own life, I experienced the beauty and joy of life more intensely when I began to pray for the ability to know and to want what God wanted for my life. As I repeated that fateful eight-word prayer, I experienced a shocking amount of peace.

My life was still chaotic. The pain of sacrifice was still real. Questions about my future still lingered. But I experienced an incredible freedom in being open to God's direction and knowing I was not going to cling too tightly to my limited vision for my life and the world. I had peace from knowing my life was in the hands of Someone – God our Father – who knows more about life, love, and happiness than I do.

At every Mass when we pray the Our Father we say "Thy Kingdom come, thy will be done, on earth as it is in heaven". These words invite us to make a choice - to choose to leave behind the all-too-familiar plans we have concocted on our own for our future.

As we pray the Our Father at the Mass, we are giving God permission to take over the broken mess of our lives, and put the broken pieces of our life together into something beautiful. During Holy Communion, we allow Jesus to enter under our roof and rearrange our life, redirect it according to God's plan, and bring healing to our soul.

However, most of the time it seems easier and more comfortable to keep doing our own thing and not be open to what God wants. And so, we pray: Lord, help me to want what you want! Thy kingdom come, thy will be done, on earth as it is in heaven!

THE LORD'S PRAYER: GIVE US THIS DAY...

Give us this day our daily bread,
and forgive us our trespasses,
as we forgive those who trespass against us;
and lead us not into temptation,
but deliver us from evil.

Maria Goretti had many reasons to be bitter.

She had a very difficult childhood. Her parents were poor sharecroppers who struggled to pay bills and feed their family. Then Maria's father died, which meant his widowed wife, Assunta Goretti, had to work long hours in the fields to provide for her family. Most of the household duties, including care of the smaller children, fell completely on Maria who was just 9 years old at the time her father died.

When Maria was 11 years old, a young man began to make sexual advances towards her. She refused these advances from 20-year old Alessandro Serenelli. Unfortunately, her daily routine of household chores and babysitting put her in close contact with Alessandro. The Serenelli family lived next door to Maria's family in a blue-collar neighborhood on the western coast of Italy. On July 5, 1902, Alessandro made another advance towards Maria and she refused by saying: "It is a sin! God does not want it!"

Filled with frustration and rage at Maria's choice not to give into his requests, Alessandro attacked and stabbed her multiple times. Eventually, assuming she was dead, he left the room. When Maria regained consciousness, she tried to open the door to call for help, but Alessandro was nearby and heard the latch open. He returned to the Goretti residence and stabbed Maria several more times.

Alessandro stabbed Maria a total of 14 times.

Later that day, Maria was found, bleeding and unconscious, on the floor of her family apartment. She was rushed to a hospital. The severity of her injuries was so grave that all attempts at preserving Maria's life were unsuccessful. However, before dying in the hospital, Maria told her family and the local priest that she forgave Alessandro.

Alessandro was arrested, convicted, and sentenced to prison for 30 years. In prison, he was known for his cruel, bitter, and violent personality. Alessandro had lived a difficult childhood and carried deep anger and frustration into his adulthood. His mother had died at a young age. One of his brothers had committed suicide. His father worked long hours to support the family and often could not give his son the attention he needed. Alessandro's prison sentence amplified his anger and his rancorous personality.

But six years into his prison sentence, Alessandro's personality began to change when he realized that Maria had actually forgiven him. Overwhelmed by the generosity of her heroic act of forgiveness, Alessandro became a devout Christian.

After his release from prison, Alessandro knocked on the door at the home of Maria's mother, Assunta Goretti, on Christmas day in 1934 and asked Assunta to forgive him. She said that since Maria had forgiven him and God had forgiven him, she forgave him as well.

This mother's act of forgiveness was incredibly heroic. After Alessandro murdered Maria, the rest of Assunta Goretti's children were placed in foster care or adopted by other families since Assunta could not care for them and work full time. Practically speaking, Alessandro had not only killed Assunta's daughter, he had taken her entire family away from her.

Both Assunta Goretti and Maria Goretti had many reasons to be bitter. Yet, they both chose to forgive Alessandro Serenelli.

These two women demonstrate the tremendous power of the words we pray during the Mass, asking God our Father to "forgive us our trespasses, as we forgive those who trespass against us". The heroic choice by Maria Goretti and Assunta Goretti to forgive Alessandro Serenelli who had trespassed against them in the most intimate and hurtful way possible, paved the way for a new beginning and change of heart in Alessandro. The choice the Gorettis made to forgive was an act of faith in God's ability to change the heart of a very sinful person. In fact, Maria's mother and Alessandro were both still alive on Saturday June 24, 1950 when the pope canonized Maria as an official Catholic saint. Alessandro spent his life after prison living with a religious community of Franciscans, in a life of prayer and service to the Church.

The parable of the prodigal son in the New Testament tells of a father who had every reason to be bitter, yet heroically chose to forgive his son who had wasted his inheritance (Luke 15:11-32). Imagine how many years of work the father must have spent earning the inheritance that his son quickly squandered on a life of dissipation, prostitutes, and foolishness. The careless behavior of this son who had become an embarrassment to his family would have crushed his father with disappointment.

And yet, the father made the heroic choice to forgive.

The forgiving father in this parable helps us understand several aspects of the words about forgiveness that we pray in the Our Father.

One lesson is that forgiveness is a free gift. We often hesitate to forgive others because we believe they do not "deserve" to be forgiven. Truth be told, from a mere human perspective, they do not deserve to be forgiven. Because of the evil they have done, what they really deserve is misery and the blunt force of our attempts at revenge.

The whole point of forgiveness, though, is that it is a gift of love. Forgiveness is not something someone can earn. Forgiveness is the choice to let go of our bitterness and desire for revenge towards those who have hurt us. Forgiveness is the choice

to pray that those who have hurt us will live better lives and become better people.

The prodigal son did not deserve a huge party. Yet, the father
chose to throw this party to demonstrate that he still loved his
son and had chosen to let go of his anger and bitterness towards
him. The party involved the best of food and drink, a band, and
dancing. This all would have been expensive, like a wedding
celebration. It would have been a party for the entire town.
The father held nothing back to make it clear to the entire community that his son was forgiven - even if the son didn't deserve
it. The father's choice to forgive was a choice of generous love.

As we pray the Lord's Prayer during the Mass, we ask God to
grant us an undeserved gift, the forgiveness of our sins. We
also ask our merciful Father to give us the strength to extend to
other people the same generous mercy that we have asked for
ourselves.

A second lesson we can learn from the story of the prodigal
son is that there should be an urgency to our willingness to forgive all those who have hurt us. The father ran to meet his way-
ward son. The father was old enough for his inheritance to be
distributed. And yet, the aged man still *runs* to meet his sinful
son and embrace him with forgiveness.

When people have hurt us, we are tempted to put off for later
the process of forgiving them. We are tempted to wait to begin
the hard work of processing the injustice others have inflicted
upon us and facing the negative feelings present in our hearts towards others. We hesitate to make the first step towards forgiveness, which is praying to God for the grace to be able to forgive.
The father's run towards his son in the parable of the prodigal
son should encourage us to refuse to procrastinate and instead
hurry towards reconciliation and forgiveness with those who
have hurt us.

The surprise ending of the prodigal son story emphasizes the
urgency with which the father embraced the task of forgiveness.
The father was the host of this huge party for his prodigal son,
and yet, leaves the party to bring about reconciliation and for-

giveness in the life of his other son who had refused to celebrate.

From a cultural perspective, to leave a party you were hosting would have been unthinkable. In modern terms, it would be like paying for a wedding reception for your daughter and then walking out before dinner is even served. People would have wondered why the father was absent from the party. It would have seemed so strange for him to be missing. There should have been nothing more urgent than the huge celebration. And yet, for the father, extending forgiveness and reconciliation to his bitter son was his top priority.

One reason we should not put off the choice to forgive is because forgiveness is a process. It takes time to understand how others have hurt us, and time to let go of the bitterness and animosity built up in our hearts. There can also be many occasions when old wounds from the past are reopened and we have to repeat the journey of forgiveness again and renew that choice to forgive the person who has hurt us.

One of the challenges, of course, is that even if we rush to forgive those who have hurt us, we may not immediately see how our forgiveness makes a positive impact in their lives. Heroic acts of forgiveness and prayers may not have an apparent effect on someone else's life until much later. In the case of Maria Goretti, the transforming power of forgiveness did not have an evident effect in the life of Alessandro until several years after her death.

The fruit of our acts of forgiveness will be something we only fully appreciate in heaven. Our Father who art in heaven challenges us to persevere in forgiveness even when we don't see immediate results. This is an act of faith in God's ability to use our deeds of forgiveness to transform the hearts of people who have hurt us into the hearts of saints. Even more importantly for us, choosing forgiveness is an act of faith that God can transform our own hearts into the hearts of saints.

Forgiveness is difficult. It can feel impossible some days. This work of mercy is only possible because of the strength we receive from our Father, who we ask at Mass to give us our "daily bread".

In the Eucharist, we receive strength from our communion with Jesus whose final moments of life were spent on the cross heroically forgiving *all* those who had rejected him, betrayed him, tortured him, and mocked him.

The Mass makes it possible for us to make the same choice to forgive, even when we have many reasons to be bitter.

THE LORD'S PRAYER: DELIVER US...

The Priest:
Deliver us, Lord, we pray, from every evil,
graciously grant peace in our days,
that, by the help of your mercy,
we may be always free from sin
and safe from all distress,
as we await the blessed hope
and the coming our Savior, Jesus Christ.
The People:
For the kingdom,
the power and the glory are yours
now and forever.

I had only been a priest for about 10 days when a man called the rectory asking for a priest to visit his house because he thought the devil had "possessed" his home.

The experienced pastor of the parish was leaving the next day for a lengthy international trip, so with a very big grin on his face he said: "This sounds like a good experience for the new priest. Take your holy water, and go visit this family tomorrow."

When I called to arrange a time to bless the home, the man told me several stories of strange phenomena taking place there. His stories made me think of scary Hollywood movies I had watched involving exorcisms.

Arriving at the "haunted house", I was nervous. The palms of my hands were sweating so my fingers stuck to the pages of my prayer book as I tried to flip to where I would begin. At a certain point in the prayers, I read a line imploring God to cleanse the home from all evil and for God to fill the home with peace.

Precisely as I read these words, a loud pounding sound came from somewhere behind me. Startled, I jumped up into the air. After my feet landed back on the ground, I continued praying even louder thinking that perhaps this noise was the devil making a dramatic exit from the home. Sweating profusely, I became more nervous.

I spoke a few more lines of the prayer when the mother of the family interrupted me. "Excuse me, father, but I think someone is knocking at the front door. Should I go answer it?"

The noise was not from the devil. It was a door-to-door salesman pounding on the wooden front door.

The salesman was sent away, and I finished the blessing without any strange phenomena occurring.

One of the main themes in the gospels is that Jesus is stronger than Satan. Jesus demonstrated this throughout his ministry, which included dramatic exorcisms.[42] However, there are other passages in the Bible which demonstrate that Satan's work is often not as dramatic as it was in these exorcisms or as depicted in scary movies.

In ancient languages the words "satan"[43] and the "devil"[44] both refer to someone who is a slanderer, someone who accuses others, someone who condemns, or someone who divides. This is the real work of Satan that we should be concerned about!

In the first pages of the Bible, Genesis chapter 3, as soon as Adam and Eve followed the advice of the evil one, they experienced division in their relationship. They both then tried to blame and accuse the other for their mistake. They no longer experienced transparency and trust in their relationship as before. Giving into temptation ruptured the bond of unity that God had established between them in truth and love.

At a certain point in Matthew's gospel, a group of Pharisees confronted Jesus as large crowds gathered around him (12:22-37). These leaders claimed that Jesus was possessed by the devil himself. They said that Jesus' extraordinary power and miraculous works were being done by an evil spirit within him.

Jesus responded to this accusation by talking about a "kingdom divided" to refer to the work Satan was doing in the world to create division and conflict among people. Jesus was insinuating to the religious leaders that their choice to create division among the people based on false accusations was a sign that they were not doing God's work but the devil's work instead. These leaders who were supposed to bring God's people together in unity and truth, were instead dividing the people of God's Kingdom by slandering, condemning, and making harsh accusations against Jesus.

The work of Satan is to divide, to slander, and to condemn.

The work of Jesus is to unite, to affirm, and to love.

Therefore, the question to ask ourselves at this point of the Mass is: Are we doing the work of Jesus or are we doing the work of the evil one?

Do our words and actions unite, affirm, and bring other people together in love and truth? Or do our words and actions divide, slander, and condemn others?

Are we uniting our hearts with the words the priest prays at this point of the Mass and allowing the Lord Jesus to purify our hearts of sinful tendencies that ultimately ruin our relationships with other people?

It is no secret that we live in a very divided and polarized world. The pain of division and slander touches each of our families, workplaces, the political world, and even religious organizations. In fact, the divisions are so great and so discouraging that it can be easy to feel like giving up. We can be tempted to give up hope of finding a better way to live. We can be tempted to give up hope that we can go beyond the backbiting, the gossip, the superficial judgmental conclusions, and the painful divisions that surround us and threaten to possess us.

This is why it is important to remember the message of the Gospel that Jesus is stronger than the evil one.

It is also vital to recognize that the purpose of the devil's work is to make us feel divided, discouraged, alone, and hopeless. This is his ultimate goal: to lead us to give up hope and to despair.

We need a closer relationship with Jesus when we are divided, discouraged, alone, condemned, and hopeless. Jesus can expose the lies of the devil that we have believed. Jesus can help us overcome the sense of helplessness, worthlessness, and despair that the devil encourages.

Jesus desires to renew within us a deep confidence in our true identity as God's beloved children and hope in our Father's promises. Isn't this what we pray for at every Mass right after the Our Father? The priest prays: "Deliver us, Lord, we pray from every evil, graciously grant peace in our days, that, by the help of your mercy we may be always free from sin and safe from all distress, as we await the blessed hope and the coming of our Savior, Jesus Christ."

These words during the Mass give us an opportunity to ask the Lord for help with all the polarized situations and divisions in our lives. This is a time during the Mass to pray for strength to rise above the cycle of gossip and slander that makes up so much of the talk around us. This is a time during the Mass to pray for the grace to resist the condemning accusations of the evil one and to find in the resurrection of Jesus a reason never to give up hope.

Satan's efforts try to lead us to give up hope and to become impatient as we await the decisive and final intervention of our Lord and Savior Jesus Christ in history. Thus, we focus our attention towards Jesus who we will receive in the Eucharist and ask him to renew our hope as he leads us to freedom from all evil. We pray that his kingdom, power, and glory may reign in us forever.

THE RITE OF PEACE

The Priest:
Lord Jesus Christ,
who said to your Apostles:
Peace I leave you, my peace I give you,
look not on our sins,
but on the faith of your Church,
and graciously grant her peace and unity
in accordance with your will.
Who live and reign for ever and ever.
The people:
Amen.
The Priest:
The peace of the Lord be with you always.
The people:
And with your spirit.
The Deacon or the Priest:
Let us offer each other the sign of peace.

Stories of war turned into stories of peace.

During the time I lived in Rome, I visited the famous Benedictine Abbey of Monte Cassino. St. Benedict founded the Monastery about 90 miles south of Rome around the year 529.

To be honest, the main reason for the visit was I needed a quiet place to study for a few days before an important graduate school exam. I was also broke at the time and the monks provided free hospitality to visiting seminarians and clergy.

The guest master was an elderly Italian priest named Father Germano. While his main job was scheduling rooms for guests and welcoming them to the monastery, he was also a font of historical knowledge. He had grown up in the area and joined the Benedictine community in the early 1940s. When World War II began, he along with several other monks had to return to their homes and stay with their families until the war was over.

Father Germano watched the horrors of World War II unfold in the previously peaceful hills where he had grown up. The area around Monte Cassino became one of the most blood-stained regions of the war. Around 55,000 members of the Allied troops lost their lives there. Around 20,000 Axis soldiers died there as well. These numbers were small compared to the even larger number of wounded on both sides.

Each day during my visit to Monte Cassino, I went for a walk after lunch with the guest master around the grounds of the monastery and he would tell me war stories. He recounted the most important battles, explaining in detail the military strategies employed by the troops and pointing out various hills and valleys where the bloody conflicts unfolded. The result of this fighting was that enough Allied forces made it through the region to be able to liberate Rome in 1944.

However, as Father Germano described the gruesome battles, he loved to share what he called "stories of shared humanity" that took place throughout the war. Some stories he had witnessed firsthand. Others he had collected from Axis and Allied soldiers who returned decades later to the monastery as tourists. The monk was quick to point out that there were more of these stories than he could count.

Most of the stories were similar. At certain points during the violent battles, troops from both sides would agree to stop fighting temporarily so that each side could give aid to the wounded and collect the bodies of their deceased comrades.

During these moments, soldiers from both sides embraced their common humanity.

Oftentimes the troops would make friendly conversation with each other using the limited phrases they knew of their opponent's native language. They would share provisions. The Allied soldiers usually shared cigarettes with the Axis soldiers.

The Axis troops usually shared chocolate, *German* chocolate, with the Allied soldiers. Father Germano related how soldiers exchanged addresses with combatants from the other side, so they could mail Christmas cards after the war. In a few situations, these "enemy" soldiers even travelled to each other's homes for friendly visits decades after the war was over.

In those brief moments of peace during a terrible war, the soldiers experienced the common humanity of the very people against whom they were fighting.

Our world needs more peace doesn't it?

As we come to Mass with hearts that are searching for greater peace, the Church directs our attention towards the Prince of Peace, the Son of God, who *chose* to become one with us in the common humanity that we share with each other.

Jesus experienced the wide range of human experiences that we experience. He had a family. He grew. He learned. He laughed. He hurt. He cried. He desired. He hungered. He thirsted. He ate. He drank. He enjoyed. He sang. He played. He loved. He worked. He suffered. He died.

God chose to become our *brother* through the humanity of Jesus Christ. God chose to become human to unite himself to *all* members of the human family.

We as Christians will discover greater peace when we begin to see other people as members of the same human family. We will live more peacefully when we are able to see in people who annoy us and frustrate us someone who shares in the same humanity as the Son of God, Jesus Christ. We will be able to love other people more, especially those who are difficult to love, if we remember that Jesus chose to die for them on the cross. Even someone who is our enemy is a member of the human family for whom Jesus died to spend eternity with in heaven.

The Son of God chose to become human to be near to even the most sinful, broken members of our human family. After many members of the human family collaborated in his torture and killing, Jesus, the Son of God, rose from the dead and reached out to his brothers and sisters in the human family, saying: "Peace be with you" (Luke 24:36; John 20:19, 21, 26).

At every Mass, the priest repeats the words of peace Jesus spoke to the human family after his resurrection. Sharing his divine peace with humanity was Jesus' response to the betrayal, hurt, mistreatment, and brokenness that he experienced in his humanity and are so common in our human experience.

During this time of the Mass, we pray for the ability to recognize the common humanity and common dignity we share with other human persons, especially those we find difficult to love: the family member who frustrates us, the co-worker who is bitter, the "friend" on social media who irritates us, the neighbor who voted for the wrong person for president, etc.

These are all people God created. All are people the Son of God became human to die for on the cross. All are people who God desires to experience mercy and salvation. All are people God can bring together in true peace.

Because of what God has done for them, they all have great dignity!

And so do we.

I wonder if one of the main reasons we struggle to find peace in our families, our country, and our world is that we do not have peace within our own hearts.

How often do we find it difficult to accept ourselves? How often do we struggle to recognize the great dignity God has given us?

How often do we tell ourselves that we are not good enough? Doubt whether we are worthy of love? Compare ourselves to others and define ourselves harshly? Question whether God really will forgive us?

This prayer for peace during the Mass invites us to discover the peace that comes from accepting the great dignity that God has given to us as his children. In creating each of us and dying on the cross for each of us, God has made it clear that we are "good enough". We are lovable and loved. We are important to someone and that Someone is God. We are sons and daughters of a Father who loves us, delights in our existence, and cherishes our friendship.

True peace is not something we earn, but rather, it is a gift that we receive from God. True unity is not possible by our own efforts alone. Peace and unity can only become a reality when we are humble enough to admit our sinfulness and ask for divine assistance to forgive and love other people.

During the Rite of Peace, we often make a gesture expressing peace, unity, and charity to those seated around us in the church building.[45] We express the peace Jesus makes possible between Christians who embrace a lifestyle of forgiveness. We celebrate the power Jesus gives us through the priest who says: "May the peace of the Lord be with you *always!*"

In the midst of a polarized and fragmented society we humbly focus our attention at Mass to the Son of God, Jesus Christ, who gives us his peace. He is the One who can show us the beauty and dignity of our common humanity. He is the One who can turn our stories of war into stories of peace.

THE FRACTION OF THE BREAD

The Priest:
May this mingling of the Body and Blood
of our Lord Jesus Christ
bring eternal life to us who receive it.

It was a really big Mass.

One particular Easter Sunday in Rome, I attended Mass at St. Peter's Square. Tens of thousands of people packed the large area in front of the church for the festive occasion.

I sat with a group of college students from Chicago who were spending a semester studying in Italy. All were Catholics who frequently attended Mass except for one female student who had never attended a Catholic Mass before. Her roommate had graciously invited her to Easter Mass that morning.

At a certain point, this young woman attending her first Mass asked: "Are all Catholic Masses like this?"

I tried not to laugh out loud at her sincere question.

I took a moment to look around at the scenery she had been taking in all morning.

The square was filled with thousands of people from every country and culture imaginable. Before Mass, Asians and Americans had been taking lots of selfies and photos for social media. Italian families had been greeting each other with lively embraces, while communicating through vivid hand gestures and vigorous chatter. An energetic group of youth from Spain had spent time before Mass singing upbeat religious songs and waving their country's flag.

All had gotten out of bed hours before dawn, waited in long security lines, and then after they passed through these security checkpoints, had sprinted to claim the seats closest to the altar. The race to claim the best seats included friendly pushing and shoving, and even some not so friendly arguments. Disputes arose over who had arrived first and earned the "rights" to certain seats.

I smiled as I turned to the young American student and explained to her that Easter Mass at St. Peter's in Rome is a very unique experience. Attending Mass elsewhere on a normal Sunday is much less intense. Typically, Catholics are not camping hours before Mass outside the church nor are they usually fighting for the front seats closest to the altar. The congregation is usually more local and not as much of a kaleidoscope of cultures and backgrounds as the crowd at Easter Mass in St. Peter's Square.

However, our Catholic belief is that each and every Mass celebrates the unity of the great diversity of peoples who make up the Church. St. Paul said: "The cup of blessing that we bless, is it not a participation in the blood of Christ? The bread that we break, is it not a participation in the body of Christ? Because the loaf of bread is one, we, though many, are one body, for we all partake of the one loaf" (1 Corinthians 10:16-17).

At Mass, we become part of something much larger than ourselves. The Eucharist integrates us into a community of believers, a body, that stretches across continents and endures throughout changes of history. The Catholic Church connects persons of all ages, from different cultures, economic classes, and educational backgrounds.

During the Communion Rite, the priest breaks into pieces the bread that has been consecrated into the Eucharistic presence of Jesus. He places one of these small pieces into the chalice. This ancient ritual has its roots in the early days of Christianity when the pope would celebrate Mass in Rome and afterwards send to each of the major churches in the city a small particle of the bread that he had consecrated into the Eucharist. Then when a priest in those churches would celebrate Mass later that day, he would place that small particle into his chalice as a way of showing the unity of his community with the pope and the larger Christian community.[46]

Today the practice of the priest fractioning the Eucharist into pieces for distribution to the faithful and placing a small particle into the chalice recalls this ancient understanding of Christian community. At Mass, we are united with the pope and the bishops whose ministry can be traced back through an unbroken line to the first apostles who celebrated the Last Supper with Jesus on the night before he died.[47] In fact, the gesture of Jesus breaking the bread at the Last Supper was so significant to the early Christians that they referred to their Sunday worship as "The Breaking of the Bread" (Acts 2:42; 20:7).[48]

The Mass is celebrated in many different places throughout the world at all hours of every day, but all Catholics who participate in this universal ritual are one in their common worship of the same God. As we enter into communion with Jesus through the Mass, Jesus draws us closer together as brothers and sisters.

When the priest places a small piece of the host into the chalice, he prays quietly: "May this mingling of the Body and Blood of our Lord Jesus Christ bring eternal life to us who receive it." These words refer to what took place on Calvary at Jesus' death. As Jesus hung on the cross on Good Friday, a soldier thrust a lance into his side, causing a stream of blood and water to flow out (John 19:34). This separation of the body and blood of Jesus at his death was overcome by God's power at his resurrection three days later. The risen Jesus appeared to his disciples in his glorified body, in flesh and blood, showing God's triumph over the forces of evil at work in the world.[49]

The words of the priest at this moment of the Mass emphasize the reality of Jesus' resurrection from the dead and the power of God to bring together what evil has divided and separated. Our reception of the Body and Blood of Christ brings with it the assurance of our own share in God's victory over evil. God has the power to overcome the effects of evil, including death – the separation of our soul and body.

While the symbolism of the Eucharist is especially vivid if we receive the host and from the chalice during Mass, we still are united fully to Jesus Christ when we receive either just the host or the chalice. We are united to Jesus Christ truly present in the Eucharist and we are united to all persons throughout the world who receive the Body and Blood of Christ in Holy Communion.

One of the beautiful aspects of being Catholic is the ability to attend Mass at any Catholic church in the world. The general format of a Roman Catholic Mass is the same in the United States as it is in other countries throughout the world. While some of the external details of the celebration might be different (style of music, church decor, etc.), the essential elements of the prayers are the same. Many of my Catholic friends have shared with me that when they attended Mass in a foreign country they were amazed that they could understand everything - even though they understood nothing. In other words, they were able to follow closely the ritual and prayers of the Mass, even though they did not understand the local language being spoken during the Mass.

The Fraction of the Bread before Communion is a good time to pray for other Christians throughout the world. It is a time to remember Catholics all over the globe who are prayerfully united to us through the Mass and the reception of the Eucharist. Family members, friends, and mentors who are geographically distant to us are actually close to us through the spiritual communion we share in Jesus through the Mass.

This is also an appropriate time to pray for Christians throughout the world who are suffering persecution and regularly risk great danger to attend the Mass. We are united to them through the Eucharist and their faithful perseverance inspires us never to take for granted the gift of the Mass that most of us attend in relative tranquility.

Through the Eucharist we are united to Catholics gathered at Mass in every possible setting imaginable: remote villages in primitive jungles, sophisticated modern cities, dangerous war zones, rural parishes, hospital chapels, high-security prisons, and St. Peter's Square in Rome. We are all one body in Christ!

Each Mass is really one big Mass.

THE LAMB OF GOD

Lamb of God, you take away the sins of the world,
have mercy on us.
Lamb of God, you take away the sins of the world,
have mercy on us.
Lamb of God, you take away the sins of the world,
grant us peace.

There is a scene from Victor Hugo's famous novel *Les Misérables* that comes to mind when I hear the phrase "Lamb of God"
that we recite together during the Mass.

Jean Valjean had spent 19 years in prison. After being released, he was unable to find a job and became destitute. One
evening the homeless, hungry man knocked at the door of a
bishop's residence and begged for help. The kind bishop invited
Jean Valjean to have dinner with him and spend the night at his
residence.

During the middle of the night, the bishop was awakened by
the police pounding at his door after they had caught Jean Valjean running away from the bishop's residence with precious silver objects. The police had caught the thief red-handed!

What happened next shocked the police and Jean Valjean. The
bishop acted as if he had given all of his silver to Jean Valjean
(the criminal) as a gift and then the bishop chastised him for dis-
obeying his orders. The bishop chided Jean Valjean for not also
taking the expensive silver candlesticks from the bishop's table
as he had instructed him.

The police and the thief were spellbound by the bishop's willingness to forgive the obvious criminal. They were stunned by
the bishop's great generosity towards a man who had attempted

to rob him and was obviously guilty of a crime.

With no further action possible against the criminal, the police exit the scene, leaving the bishop and Jean Valjean alone together. The bishop took this opportunity to encourage Jean Valjean to do good with what he had received as a generous and free gift.

As the story continues, it becomes clear that this free gift and act of mercy from the bishop was the turning point in Jean Valjean's life. The grace of this moment lifted him out of his despair and sinful tendencies. The undeserved generosity of the bishop moved him to use his life to do good for others and to contribute to the good of society.

In the Old Testament, God's people made many attempts to express sorrow for their sinfulness. Over and over again, they tried to do something for God to express regret for being unfaithful. They would acknowledge their guilt by sacrificing an animal, oftentimes a lamb, as a way of saying: "Because of our unfaithfulness, we deserve to die like this animal". They were acknowledging that they deserved to die because of their ingratitude and their unfaithfulness towards God who had created them, given them life, and cared for them in so many different ways.

Despite these animal sacrifices, the people still felt guilt. They still struggled to show faithfulness to God. The peace they sought in their hearts still remained inaccessible to them.

The Son of God came to earth to free God's people from the guilt they experienced deep within their souls. Jesus sacrificed himself on the cross to give them a peace that their animal sacrifices could never bring. Jesus carried humanity across the gulf of eternal separation from God that it deserved because of its frequent and blatant rejection of God throughout history. Jesus did all of this as a free and generous gift to undeserving humanity.

During the Mass, we repeat the words "Lamb of God" several times to refer to Jesus who is present under the appearance of bread and wine. Jesus died on the cross to take away the guilt of our sins and to make it possible for our hearts to be filled with his peace.[50] The Lamb of God prayers during the Mass are a time to ask for God's mercy and to pray for the gift of God's peace to fill our souls. We especially give thanks for the forgiveness of sins we have experienced through the sacraments of Baptism and Reconciliation.

This is also a time to pray for God's mercy on all sinners. We pray during the Mass for even the worst of sinners. They lack peace within their own souls. They have often experienced deep hurt in their lives. We pray that the Lamb of God might show mercy to them, inspire them to change their ways, and grant them peace.

We are also praying that we might be able to share God's mercy and peace with other people, including those who have hurt us in very significant ways. The undeserved mercy we have received from God is a gift we are meant to share with others.

What is perhaps most interesting about Victor Hugo and Les Mis is that the author was not a big fan of Catholicism. In fact, he was highly critical of Catholicism. After Victor Hugo's own son read a draft of the story, he critiqued his father for portraying a Catholic bishop in such a positive light in Les Mis. His response to his son is very thought provoking.

Victor Hugo said this image of a generous, merciful Catholic clergyman was meant to be a criticism of the Church of that time. Clergy in those days were not known for being rich in mercy, forgiveness, or charity. The depiction in Les Mis of such a saintly Catholic was meant to be satire.[51]

As we recite the Lamb of God, we pray that the words we speak during Mass do not become satire in our own lives. We pray that we will be conduits of God's mercy and peace to others. We pray that we might generously share the free gift of mercy that the Lamb of God has bestowed upon us.

COMMUNION

As a child, I believed my grandfather could do anything.

I grew up in a family with six male children, which meant we were constantly breaking things around the house. The standard procedure was that if you broke something you would wait for dad to get home from work and see if he could fix it. If dad could not fix it, we would take it to grandpa's shop the next day because grandpa could fix anything.

No matter what it was or how badly it was broken, grandpa could fix it.

It seemed like when grandpa put his mind to it, he could do anything. As a teenager, he drove landing barges in the Mediterranean Sea during World War II. After the war, he founded a successful family business.

A few days after I was ordained a priest, I was at my parent's home opening congratulatory cards from the ordination. As I began to read the handwritten message in one of these cards, I stopped after the first line to look down to see who had signed it. What had peaked my curiosity was that the handwriting was incredibly sloppy and the spelling was atrocious.

I expected to see the signature of a student from an elementary school at one of the parishes where I had served as a seminarian. The penmanship and grammar were so bad I assumed only a child could have written such a message in the card.

However, at the bottom of the card, I found the name of an 85-year-old man:

Ralph A. Smith

Grandpa

In that moment, I remembered something my grandfather had told me dozens of times. His formal schooling ended during 7th grade after receiving what he called "a master's degree in spit wad shooting". This was his fun way of urging his grandchildren to appreciate their education, since he only had the opportunity to complete 6 years of school before working full-time to support his family, struggling through the Great Depression.

Reading that ordination card made it very clear that my grandpa could not do everything. He could barely write, spell, or read. I went back to the top of the card and read his message that had taken so much effort to write on my ordination day:

When you come to a hill that you can't climb
Remember you [are] not alone

"Climb" was misspelled with a "k": k-l-i-m-e. The last phrase was missing the verb ("are"). He had written "Alone" as two words "A Lone". Many letters and words were crossed out and rewritten, with the final version of some words still spelled incorrectly.

Despite the misspellings and the abundant crossing-outs and corrections grandpa had made, the meaning was clear. In his own way, grandpa's message summarized an important lesson of Catholic theology: There are some challenges that we cannot overcome on our own.

During the Communion Rite, the priest quietly recites a special prayer prior to receiving Holy Communion. The content of this prayer focuses on achievements in our spiritual journey that we cannot attain on our own. This prayer of preparation for Holy Communion asks Jesus for divine help in climbing the insurmountable mountains that threaten to block us from eternal salvation. In particular, the priest prays for help overcoming his sinfulness, the power of the Satan, and death itself.

The priest has a choice between two different prayers of preparation for Holy Communion. The themes are similar. The prayers ask Jesus for his divine mercy, divine strength against temptation, and divine protection from all evil. Ultimately, these prayers ask for the gift of eternal salvation, a reality that we as sinners cannot achieve on our own.

While the Church does not give lay persons prescribed formulas to pray during this moment of the Mass, themes of the priest's prayer can provide some focus during this time of preparation for Holy Communion. As you prepare for Holy Communion, ask for Jesus' help with the insurmountable mountains you are facing in your life. Ask for Jesus' assistance with particular temptations you find to be challenging. Ask for Jesus to remedy your sinful tendencies and deep insecurities. Ask for the undeserved gift of eternal salvation in heaven.

The priest's prayer signals that this is a time in the Mass of intense preparation for union with God. We pray that our union with Jesus will last forever. The priest begs Jesus in his prayer: "never let me be parted from you". Before we receive communion, we ask Jesus to stay with us on our journey and guide us through every difficult situation we face until heaven.

Our preparation for communion is a time for us to focus on what my grandfather wrote on my ordination day:

When you come to a hill that you can't climb
Remember you [are] not alone

BEHOLD THE LAMB OF GOD...

The Priest:
Behold the Lamb of God,
behold him who takes away the sins of the world.
Blessed are those called to the supper of the Lamb.

It was not the message they expected.

It was graduation day. Seniors at Calvert High School in Tiffin, Ohio were wearing their royal blue caps and gowns. Parents, grandparents, and family were out in full force. Many held large cameras ready to capture memories of this special day.

The commencement speaker was an esteemed teacher attending his final graduation as a member of the school faculty. Revered as an excellent educator, he was also known as a wise, entertaining orator.

Most of us expected his message to be the typical "feel good" speech usually delivered on these sorts of occasions. We thought he would say that memories from high school will be special for a lifetime, that graduates should follow their dreams, and that the future would bring success.

However, one of the main points of his commencement address was not what people were expecting to hear that warm afternoon. It did not seem to fit with the "feel good" theme of the day.

The speaker told the graduates that they needed to learn something very important.

What was this nugget of wisdom to remember for the rest of their lives?

The speaker summarized this precious piece of advice in two short sentences: "Life is not fair and life is hard. *Deal with it!*"

Some of the students shifted nervously in their seats. Many parents and grandparents put their cameras down to focus on the speaker. They knew what he said was true. Life is not always fair. Life can be very hard sometimes.

It seemed to be a harsh message for such a happy day.

But looking back, the scene reminds me of the day Jesus preached his famous sermon that we now refer to as the Beatitudes (Matthew 5:1-12).

Teaching on a beautiful hillside by the sea of Galilee, Jesus used words that were poetic and beautiful. And yet, if we really listen to the Beatitudes, they are startling and pointed. Jesus' words were not necessarily the "feel good" message that many in the crowd probably expected him to preach.

Jesus described a "blessed" life very differently than most of us would. He described a hard life, filled with unfairness and difficulty as "blessed"!

Scrolling through social media, the word "blessed" is something we see if people are feeling good: #blessed. We tag photos on Facebook or Instagram as #blessed when we have a wonderful meal with family and friends, take a great vacation, receive a promotion at work, or something else pleasant happens to us.

However, in the Beatitudes, Jesus defined being blessed to mean something very different.

He said that we are blessed when we are sad and mourn. When life makes us cry.

Jesus said that we are blessed when people insult us and treat us unfairly.

Jesus said that we are blessed when there is conflict among our family, roommates, coworkers, or friends and we need to serve as peacemakers.

Jesus said that we are blessed when we are spiritually weak – "poor in spirit" – and realize we cannot be virtuous by our own power.

Jesus said that we are blessed when the world is in chaos and we find ourselves hungering and thirsting for a more just and righteous world.

Jesus said that we are blessed when others hurt us and give us opportunities to be merciful.

Can you imagine how strange it would look on social media if we started sharing our being #blessed in these ways?

Very strange, indeed, because we would be posting pictures of all the hard, difficult, and unfair moments of life and defining them as "blessed" experiences. Most people would probably think we were being cynical or sarcastic.

Yet, Jesus taught us that we have reason to say we are blessed when life is hard, difficult, and unfair. Why? How?

Why did Jesus tell us that we are blessed even when suffering physically, emotionally, or spiritually? When life brings us tears, insults, conflicts, and unjust circumstances?

The answer to the "why" and "how" behind the Beatitudes is an incredibly consoling message.

We are blessed even when life is unfair and hard because Jesus taught us that there is more to life than physical health, material wealth, glamourous appearances, and the opinions of other people.

We are blessed even when life is difficult because Jesus makes it possible for us to love even in the worst of circumstances.

We are blessed even when life is ugly because love and the beauty of love can shine even brighter when darkness completely surrounds us.

We are blessed even when life is burdensome because Jesus, the Good Shepherd, is leading us through this valley of tears towards the unending joy and peace of heaven.

We can even say we are blessed when sin disfigures our world and our own hearts, because Jesus is the Lamb of God who takes away the sins of the world.

The Beatitudes teach us not to give into a trend in religious thinking that was common in Jesus' time and is very popular in our own time. A "prosperity gospel" that promises comfort here and now in this world if we are faithful to God is certainly very appealing. Yet, Jesus clearly predicted that life on earth, at times, will be difficult if we follow him.

If we are looking for a Savior who will make life easy on earth, then Jesus is not the one to follow. Jesus is a Savior who came to bring us eternal salvation and make it possible for us to share in a relationship with God that lives on into eternity. Jesus came to lead us to heaven, not to guarantee us earthly comfort.

This truth is communicated to us as the priest elevates the host prior to the distribution of Holy Communion and says "blessed are those called to the supper of the Lamb". We are blessed to be at Mass, not because Jesus is guaranteeing us a comfortable, easy life here on earth. Rather, we are blessed because our true destiny is heaven.

In the last book of the Bible, the Book of Revelation, the phrase "wedding feast of the Lamb" refers to the life of heaven (Revelation 19:9). The Mass is a foretaste and preview of this heavenly banquet. At Mass, we encounter Jesus, the Lamb of God, who takes away our sins and makes it possible for us one day to spend eternity celebrating God's presence in heaven. Thus, the priest echoes the words of the Book of Revelation during the Mass: "Blessed are those called to the supper of the Lamb".

In other words, we are truly "blessed" to be able to participate in the Mass not because God has promised to take away all of our earthly problems, but rather, because at Mass our hope is renewed in heaven and Jesus reassures us that the sin-filled world in which we live is not our ultimate destiny. Our destiny is to be wedded with God forever in heaven. God's plan will be consummated in an unbreakable bond of love that will bring us eternal joy in heaven.

We are truly blessed!

Life *is* unfair and hard, but because of Jesus we have a reason for hope, and so we can deal with it!

However, following Jesus now will require us to make some difficult choices.

In the first chapter of John's gospel, a group of people faced a very difficult choice. They had to decide whether or not to embrace a hard path.

John the Baptist was spending time with his followers when Jesus came toward them. John pointed out Jesus as the One sent from God to take away the sins of the world. He told his followers that Jesus was greater than he and that Jesus was the Son of God. John the Baptist said: "Behold, the Lamb of God, who takes away the sin of the world" (John 1:29).

John was telling his closest companions and friends that it was time for them to leave him. To depart from John and follow Jesus instead.

Imagine the natural hesitation of John the Baptist's followers. They had become close to him. His teaching had made a difference in their lives. The baptism he celebrated with them gave them an experience of repentance and God's forgiveness. John had given them hope.

Why should they leave to follow another teacher? Why leave a well-established, well-respected, and genuine prophet to follow a man whom they knew hardly anything about? To follow a man who had spent the past couple decades working as a carpenter in an obscure village of Galilee?

Apparently, none of John the Baptist's followers made a move to follow Jesus. The gospel of John makes no mention of anyone leaving John to follow Jesus that day.

However, if we keep reading in the gospel of John, we find that the next day Jesus again approached John the Baptist and his disciples. John the Baptist *again* pointed out Jesus with the words: "Behold, the Lamb of God" (John 1:36).

After a night of thinking about what John the Baptist had told them, what would they do? We can imagine they had tossed and turned all night, pondering if they should leave the man and the place that had been so important to them.

Now Jesus was standing in front of them. He was giving them a second chance. Would they follow him as John the Baptist had encouraged them?

Two of John's many disciples took a leap of faith and followed Jesus that day.

One was Andrew, who went and found his brother, Simon Peter. They began to follow Jesus together.

The rest is history.

They became some of Jesus' first apostles and eventually very important leaders in the Church.

Being open to understanding and following God's plan for our lives can be difficult because it often means making the same decision as the followers of John the Baptist. They had to make a leap of faith. They had to allow Jesus to be their God who would determine the future path of their lives. They had to be willing to follow in Jesus' footsteps and embrace a life of sacrificial love that included suffering.

At each Mass the same choice is put before each of us as the priest says: "Behold the Lamb of God, behold him who takes away the sins of the world". At this moment, we have the opportunity to choose to follow Jesus and to allow him to determine the future path of our lives.

Most of us experience some fear when we truly recognize what following Jesus means for our future. We know that following Jesus will bring us the blessedness of the Beatitudes and not the blessedness of earthly comfort or pleasure. We recognize we will have to give up the comfort of our sinful, selfish habits if we allow Jesus to take away our sins and direct our future path. As we contemplate the Lamb of God, present under the appearance of the broken host held up before us, we are faced with a gut-check moment. Jesus waits for a response. Will I be vulnerable and open myself up entirely to him during Holy Communion? Will I hold nothing back from him? Will I allow him to influence all areas of my life?

Our response at this moment of the Mass is a time for us to imitate the bold response of saints like Andrew and Simon Peter. This is a time to ask Jesus to take over our lives and direct our futures. This is a time to acknowledge how blessed we are to be invited to the celebration of heaven.

LORD, I AM NOT WORTHY...

All:
Lord, I am not worthy
that you should enter under my roof,
but only say the word
and my soul shall be healed.

One big drunken mess.

The Sistine Chapel in Vatican City contains some of the most famous artwork in the world. Its walls and ceiling are covered in spectacular paintings created by the talented brushstrokes of Michelangelo.

The legendary artist painted stories from the Book of Genesis on the ceiling of the Sistine Chapel. They are the sorts of beautiful images that frequently appear in religion textbooks or prayer books.

They tell the story of God's creation of the world and his creation of Adam and Eve. Michelangelo painted the bodies of Adam and Eve to appear almost superhuman, with overwhelming beauty, perfect form, and unmistakable strength. The artist was clearly indicating that God created humanity to reflect God's glory in the world. Humanity was created in the image and likeness of God.

However, the last painting on the ceiling is one that most people never have seen. It is not the sort of picture you find in prayer books or religion textbooks. The shocking image is a startling contrast to the glory of humanity shown in the first few paintings on the ceiling.

It is the story of one big drunken mess.

At the end of the ceiling in the Sistine Chapel is the story from the Book of Genesis about the day when Noah (who built the ark) got embarrassingly drunk on wine. Michelangelo depicted Noah laying on the ground, naked, completely passed out from his drinking. Noah's children surround him and try to figure out what to do in this shameful and embarrassing situation.

This painting comes as a sad, shocking ending to the story of creation that, up to this point, had showed how God intended to reveal his beauty and glory through humanity. Michelangelo appears to be saying with this image: "In the end, humanity is one big drunken mess. In the end, humanity's weakness and brokenness is exposed. In the end, we can't help but embarrass ourselves and bring shame upon ourselves despite the glorious destiny the Creator had intended for us."

While some of us may have never heard of this story about Noah from the Old Testament (Genesis 9), it is a story that we all know well from our life experience.

We know the brokenness of our human condition.

We know the weakness of our humanity that finds itself getting drunk not just on wine, but also drunk with pride, with greed, with lust, and with selfishness. Humanity creates one big drunken mess, as we fixate on earthly pleasures, earthly power, and earthly possessions in such an excessive way that it leads to embarrassing and shameful actions.

Because of humanity's selfish obsessions, our world is a very painful place to live.

In fact, the world is so painful that we find ourselves in a vicious cycle that tempts us to despair and purposefully find a way to "pass out" and numb ourselves to the pain of life. We are tempted to do anything necessary to avoid facing the overwhelming pain of our problems here on earth.

We really wish earth would be a happier place. That our human existence could be filled with the beauty and glory God intended when creating Adam and Eve in the garden of Eden. That we could live the joy of the abundant life God intended for us in the beginning.

That we could go beyond the big drunken mess.

And yet, we know that our human efforts alone are unable to change things. We need divine help to change this sinful condition ruining our lives.

In the Communion Rite, we pray: "Lord, I am not worthy that you should enter under my roof, but only say the word and my soul shall be healed." These words are based upon the request a Roman centurion made to Jesus in the New Testament (Matthew 8:8; Luke 7:6-7). The soldier trusted in Jesus' power, but was deeply aware of his own sinfulness and the sinfulness of his household.

As a Roman soldier, he would have been part of a ruthless dictatorship that treated power as a god. Roman soldiers enforced with violence the orders they received. They knew how selfish and arbitrary human choices can be made. They saw firsthand how human life can be treated cheaply. They knew how much pain and misery selfishness can cause in the world.

This Roman solider understood that his power alone or the power of any normal human being could not stop the merciless reign of evil in the world.

During the Mass, we pray for healing from the sickness of soul that the reign of evil has caused in each of us.

We need Jesus' healing power to change our hearts and to renew them with the goodness that God first breathed into us when we were created. We need Jesus' healing power to transform our lives that have been wounded and hurt by sinful people. We need Jesus' healing power to transform humanity that is drunk with power and selfishness, so that humanity can learn to love, to share, and to give again. We need Jesus' healing power to touch us so that we can be more than one big drunken mess.

We make the Roman centurion's words our own during the Mass as an act of humility, acknowledging we need Jesus' healing work for our salvation.[52] We give Jesus permission to rearrange our life, upend our selfish tendencies, and reorganize

our priorities. We consent to let go of our lifestyle of self-grati-
fication, and allow Jesus to enter under our roof to lead us in the
way of the Beatitudes.

In the Sistine Chapel, the image of the drunk, naked, passed
out Noah is the last story on the ceiling. However, right below
that image begins a row of several paintings of Old Testament
prophets.

As your eye follows this row of prophets around the room, you
eventually arrive at the focal point of the chapel, Michelangelo's
dramatic painting of the last judgment that stands over the
altar. At the center is an image of the Son of God in human flesh.

This image of Jesus Christ is rather powerful. By powerful, I
mean physically powerful.

Jesus is so buff that it looks like he works out 6 to 8 hours per
day with a personal trainer and only eats lean protein and super-
foods like kale and quinoa.

This image of human, bodily perfection is intentional.

Jesus' human perfection is a sign of hope and challenge for
sinful humanity.

His glorious humanity shows that it is possible for humanity
to live the glory and beauty of human life that God created us for
in the beginning. Despite humanity's sinful past, we see in Jesus
that humanity can live the beautiful life of trust, love, and generosity that the Creator planned for us.

Despite our own human weakness, Jesus makes it possible for
us through Holy Communion to share in his strength, wisdom,
and courage.

During this prayer of the Mass, we admit our own sinfulness,
our own brokenness, and our own selfishness. We also acknowledge that we have a reason to have hope. That there is a divine
physician who can restore us to true life. We ask Jesus to heal us
from our habit of committing particular sins. We request that
our union with the glorified humanity of Jesus in Holy Communion will empower us to fulfill the purpose for which God created us.

Because of our union with Him, we can become something

much better than one big drunken mess.

MAY THE BODY OF CHRIST...

The Priest:
May the Body of Christ
keep me safe for eternal life.
The Priest:
May the Blood of Christ
keep me safe for eternal life.
The minister of Communion:
The Body of Christ.
The communicant:
Amen.
The minister of Communion:
The Blood of Christ.
The communicant:
Amen.

"We took each other for granted."

A parishioner who had recently gone through a divorce requested to speak with me. He began our conversation sharing many examples of successes he and his wife had accomplished during their 25+ years of marriage. They had successfully raised several children and achieved success in their professional careers. He spoke about their financial success and the affluence they had accumulated. Their active social life had successfully forged connections with many important persons. They had successfully integrated volunteer work into their busy schedules as well.

After listing their many successes as a married couple, the

man got to the main problem that had led to their divorce.

He summarized it by simply stating: "We took each other for granted."

The couple so fixated on being successful in so many areas of life that, without even realizing at the time, they began taking each other for granted. Early on in their marriage, they stopped acknowledging sacrifices they were making for each other. They stopped being grateful for the little things that often end up being the most meaningful things within marriage. They seldom took time to appreciate the presence of their spouse. They rarely spent quality time together.

Taking each other for granted eventually led to a relationship that lacked depth, emotional connection, intimacy, mutual understanding, and a shared vision for the future. The distance that grew between them led to some regrettable decisions that brought one of them to file for divorce.

At the end of our conversation, the man said to me: "Father, when you prepare couples for marriage please share my story with them. Tell them not to take their friendship with their spouse for granted."

Sadly, I'm afraid this man's story is somewhat typical. We tend to take the most important relationships in our lives for granted.

The Rite of Communion during Mass can be a time when this tendency can play itself out quite frequently. It is a time when we can be tempted to take our relationship with Jesus and his loving presence for granted.

One reason we become easily distracted during this part of the Mass is because often a good deal of movement is taking place: persons assisting with the distribution of communion line up around the sanctuary, they receive communion, and go stand at their communion stations. Then the communion lines start moving, we take part in the communion procession, then we find our seat again, etc.

The danger here is that we can go through most of this time without hardly praying at all. We can easily go through the motions of the Rite of Communion (when our attention span is already mostly spent) and take Jesus' presence for granted.

Practically speaking, the Rite of Communion takes 10 or 15 minutes at most parishes on Sunday, which is actually about 20 to 25% of the entire time we spend at Sunday Mass!

There are many ways to make the most your time during the Rite of Communion. Talk to Jesus about what is going on in your life. Ask his help with your needs. Give thanks and count your blessings. Sing to him using words from a hymn of praise or a chant that the choir is singing. Pray for other people. Or simply be silent, resting joyfully in the awareness that you are loved by Jesus and that he has chosen to enter into an eternal friendship with you.

We say "Amen" as we receive Holy Communion as a way of saying "so be it", "yes, I accept this commitment Jesus is making to me", "yes, I choose to enter into communion with Jesus who I believe is truly present here", "yes, I entrust my life to Jesus working through the Church today".

The prayers surrounding reception of Holy Communion highlight the lasting significance of this moment. Participating at Mass can feel routine, especially as mundane concerns compete for our attention, but the effects of receiving Holy Communion are long-term. They are eternal.

Before the priest consumes the host, he prays quietly: "May the Body of Christ keep me safe for eternal life". Before drinking from the chalice, the priest prays: "May the Blood of Christ keep me safe for eternal life." Through these prayers, the priest acknowledges that mere human efforts alone cannot save us from a sinful destiny. Our union with the Son of God, the risen Jesus, in Holy Communion makes it possible for us to share in the eternal life of heaven.

For several centuries, the words the priest now prays quietly before receiving Holy Communion were words that he prayed while distributing Holy Communion to each member of the faithful. He would say to each person: "May the Body of our Lord Jesus Christ preserve your soul unto life everlasting." These

MAY THE BODY OF CHRIST... 181

words alerted the faithful to the tremendous, eternal consequences of their union with Jesus in Holy Communion. Early Christians called the Eucharist the "medicine of immortality" for this reason.[53] Holy Communion provides divine strength to fight against sin, keeping us safe from Satan's attempts to bully us into forfeiting the gift of salvation promised at our Baptism. Frequent reception of the Eucharist is a great practical help in overcoming temptation.

When received in the final moments of life, Holy Communion is called *viaticum*.[54] In the ancient world, this Latin expression referred to provisions (food, money, etc.) of a traveler. The Church refers to the Eucharist as *viaticum* since it is the food that sustains us on our journey to heaven. Jesus, present in the Eucharist, leads Christians on their journey through the most difficult moments of life, including death. Because of the presence of Jesus in the Eucharist as viaticum, Christians are never alone, never separated from love, no matter how dark or evil the circumstances.

On days when you don't feel like going to Mass or are distracted during the Communion Rite, consider the sacrifices made by Christians who walk many miles on unpaved trails in rural Africa to celebrate Mass whenever a priest is within several hours of their village. Ponder the faith of the early Christians who risked their lives to attend Mass secretly in the dark of night. Think of the prisoners' devotion in concentration camps and work camps in the 20th century who risked torture and death for the sake of receiving a tiny crumb of the Eucharist.

One such prisoner, Father Walter Ciszek, recounted that during decades spent in tortuous Soviet work camps, Catholic prisoners regularly sacrificed food or sleep to attend a Mass celebrated secretly at night or during a meal period. Of course, if prison guards discovered them, they would have been punished severely or simply killed. Father Ciszek described his experience of the Mass in a brutal Siberian workcamp this way:

> In every camp, the priests and prisoners would go to
> great lengths, run risks willingly, just to have the con-

solation of this sacrament…In small groups the prison-
ers would shuffle into the assigned place, and there the
priest would say Mass in his working clothes, unwashed,
disheveled, bundled up against the cold. We said
Mass in drafty storage shacks, or huddled in mud and
slush in the corner of a building site foundation of an
underground. The intensity of devotion of both priests
and prisoners made up for everything; there were no
altars, candles, bells, flowers, music, snow-white linens,
stained glass or warmth that even the simplest parish
church could offer. Yet in these primitive conditions, the
Mass brought you closer to God than anyone might con-
ceivably imagine. The realization of what was happen-
ing on the board, box, or stone used in place of an altar
penetrated deep into the soul. Distractions caused by
the fear of discovery, which accompanied each saying
of the Mass under such conditions, took nothing away
from the effect that tiny bit of bread and few drops of
consecrated wine produced upon the soul.[55]

These Christians understood who they were receiving in Holy Communion.

To avoid taking for granted what is happening in the Rite of Communion, we should prepare for communion by consciously calling to mind who we will be receiving – Jesus, the Son of God. The same Jesus who healed the sick with compassion. Cured the blind with divine power. Touched lepers with care. Raised the dead. Forgave terrible sinners. Patiently taught his friends. Courageously spoke the truth. Suffered torture and died on the cross for us. Rose from the dead. Ascended into glory in heaven and chose us to carry on his work here on earth.

This is who is uniting himself to us through Holy Communion! Call to mind Jesus' love, compassion, courage, humility, divine power, and human affection when you pray at this special time during the Mass. Marvel at this privilege the Son of God chooses to give you. He chooses you to be his friend! He is leading *you* to be with him forever in heaven.

This is a friendship we should never take for granted.

WHAT HAS PASSED OUR LIPS...

The Priest:
What has passed our lips as food, O Lord,
may we possess in purity of heart,
that what has been given to us in time
may be our healing for eternity.

The Priest:
Let us pray.

The people:
Amen.

There are only a few people who ever stop and look up, but those who do are not disappointed.

Millions of people visit St. Peter's Basilica in Rome each year. During my time living in Rome, I would frequently see a long line of tourists waiting to enter the church. Most would wait in line 30 minutes, 45 minutes, or more than an hour to get inside.

People visit St. Peter's because of its rich history, magnificent architecture, and important spiritual significance. From an artistic perspective, the church is filled with literally tons of inspiring and noteworthy pieces of artwork. There are famous pieces of artwork like Michelangelo's Pieta statue, carvings by Bernini, mosaics inspired by famous artists like Raphael, and many other mosaics, statues, and sculptures that make the Basilica certainly one of the most beautiful churches in the world.

However, my favorite piece of artwork is something that probably 99% of visitors miss. In a very strange place, most people fail to notice that it is even there.

This mosaic is inside the front entryway of the church, near the ceiling. It is located above the front gate, which means that the only time when you could possibly notice this mosaic is when exiting the church.

There are lots of reasons why people fail to notice this picture when exiting the church. Their gaze is often drawn into the piazza (the square) filled with hundreds of tourists from all over the world. Some visitors are passionately discussing the scrumptious Italian cuisine they will soon eat. Other tourists are looking down at their phones or cameras reviewing photos they have just captured. They are all too distracted. Very few people stop and look up several feet to the top of the tall gate to see this special mosaic on their way out of the church.

This special mosaic is a depiction of a gospel story. In Matthew 14:22-33, Peter was in a boat with the other disciples on the Sea of Galilee when harsh winds and strong waves started tossing the boat in the sea. Jesus appeared and said to the disciples, "Take courage, it is I; do not be afraid". Jesus then invited Peter to come to him on the water. Peter accepted this invitation and began to walk on the water towards Jesus, but then, after getting scared by the storm, sunk into the sea. In his fear and panic, Peter called out to Jesus "Lord, save me!" Jesus stretched out his hand, caught Peter, and said to him: "O you of little faith, why did you doubt?"

During my first guided tour of St. Peter's Basilica, I learned there is a specific purpose behind the placement of this story above the front gate. The designers of the basilica knew this story could teach a very important lesson to Christians exiting the church after Mass. They knew these Christians would face challenges, problems, and scary situations in their lives.

This scene teaches us that as we exit a church building, we should fight to keep our focus and our attention on Jesus. Focusing only on our problems and our difficulties, will lead us to sink like Simon Peter. The proper Christian approach to the storms of life is to focus on Jesus, who says to us: "Take courage, it is I; do not be afraid".

These words are particularly helpful for our reflection during the Rite of Communion. The purpose of our reception of Holy Communion is not just a few moments of special encounter with Jesus within the church building. Rather, our encounter with Jesus during Mass should lead us to lean on him and continue our communion with him as we exit the church and go into the world.

As the priest or deacon is cleansing the vessels used during the distribution of Holy Communion, he prays a special prayer asking that the Eucharist we have received as spiritual food might transform our souls and heal us of our tendency to fall into sin. The image of the vessels being cleansed is a fitting image of what the Eucharist does within our souls. It purifies us. The Eucharist helps us overcome temptation, especially strong temptations we experience when stressed, tired, and tossed about by the challenges of life outside the walls of the church building.

Peter would have been very tired in the scene depicted over the door of St. Peter's in Rome. That night came right after the day when Jesus fed 5,000 people with the help of his disciples (Matthew 14:13-22). After this intense day, the disciples had gotten into a boat and tried to cross to the other side. The gospel of Matthew says that it was in the fourth watch of the night when this encounter between Jesus and Peter took place (Matthew 14:25). The fourth watch of the night was the time period from 3 AM to 6 AM. It would have been super late! Further, this trip across the lake should have been routine and easy, but was actually very difficult because the wind was against the disciples. It was a tiring and frustrating journey at the end of a day that already had been intense and draining. By the fourth watch of the night, the disciples should have reached the other side. The strong winds left the disciples frustrated, defeated, and just plain worn out.

In this moment of stress and frustration and fatigue, Peter took his attention from Jesus' presence and instead gave into the temptation of despair, sinking into the water. During the Prayer After Communion, we ask for the strength to keep our attention on Jesus during moments of temptation. We are praying that because of what has happened at the Mass, we will not allow the storms of earthly life to lead us into despair.

The priest's words "Let us pray" at the end of the Rite of Communion are similar to the words introducing the Collect at the beginning of Mass. This time of prayer is designed to bring together all the prayers offered by the community during the Rite of Communion. The words the priest vocalizes from *The Roman Missal* are typically somewhat generic, since the purpose is to unite all the personal prayers we have offered to God during the Rite of Communion. The Prayer After Communion focuses our attention on Jesus' presence that we have just received and asks that his presence will make a lasting impact on our lives.[56]

The Prayer after Communion concludes the Rite of Communion. Then the final stage of the Mass begins. The Concluding Rites empower us for our divine mission outside the church building. When try to live our faith in the world, there will be disappointments and setbacks. There will be times when we will be frustrated with ourselves and with others. At times, the powers of hell will throw their worst at us to scare and intimidate us. Yet, we do not need to panic. We simply need to keep our attention focused on Jesus who has chosen to unite himself to us through Holy Communion. He is stronger than anything the storms of life and the powers of hell can throw at us.

THE CONCLUDING RITES: THE BLESSING AND THE DISMISSAL

The Priest:
The Lord be with you.
The people:
And with your spirit.
The Priest:
May almighty God bless you,
the Father, and the Son, and the Holy Spirit.
The People:
Amen.
The Deacon or Priest:
Go forth, the Mass is ended.
Or
Go and announce the Gospel of the Lord.
Or
Go in peace, glorifying the Lord by your life.
Or
Go in peace.

This is one of those moments at Mass when we very easily become totally distracted.

Where will we go to brunch or what we will eat when we get home?

What is planned for the rest of the day?

Where did we park? How far we will have to walk to reach our vehicle?

What's the page number of the last song in the hymnal?

Distractions are definitely the norm during the Concluding Rites at the end of Mass, even though this should be one of the most powerful moments in our week.

The blessing at the end of the Mass is a continuation of the blessing Jesus prayed with his disciples before he ascended into heaven. The gospel of Luke narrates how Jesus "raised his hands, and blessed them. As he blessed them he parted from them and was taken up to heaven" (Luke 24:50-51).

The verb "to bless", *benedicere* in Latin and *eulogein* in Greek (like eulogy), means "to speak well of" or "to call good". Thus, at the end of Mass the words of blessing are a declaration that the all-knowing, all-powerful, eternal God sees good in you. Through the voice of the priest, God is declaring that we are good! God is affirming the good that is in us. The blessing at the end of Mass, re-echoes God's delight recorded in the first paragraphs of the Book of Genesis: "God looked at everything he had made, and found it very good" (Genesis 1:31).

As we leave Mass, the blessing reminds us that we are good people! Yes, we all have our flaws. Yes, all of us are imperfect. Yes, we are each a work in progress. At the core of our being though, God sees good in us and declares that we are *very* good! The blessing at the end of the Mass proclaims that each of us is precious, valuable, and treasured by God despite our weaknesses and sinfulness that God knows so well. It is good that we exist!

This is important to keep in mind as we leave church and go out into the world. While there will be moments when we all fail to live up to our divine mission, God still commissions us to do his work in the world.

It is through the final words of the Mass that Jesus commissions us and sends us forth to do his work. At the end of Sunday Mass, Jesus says to us through the deacon or priest: "Go!"

Go! Leave the church building! Go out and live your faith! Share your faith! Serve others! Help other people experience the good news of salvation!

The priest's or deacon's final words at the end of Sunday Mass are not just a polite reminder that our time in church is finished. Rather, they are a solemn proclamation that God has chosen each of us to do a specific task and fulfill a unique mission in the world.

God calls each of us to fulfill an *irreplaceable* role in the world. Whether mothers or fathers, married people without children, single, religious sisters or brothers, widowed, children, we are all sent forth at the end of Mass to do God's work in the world.

What Jesus did on the day of the Ascension was rather bold. He entrusted his mission to us. Jesus disappeared from this earth as he ascended into heaven and assigned us weak, human beings with the task of making him visible in the world.

After we receive the real presence of Jesus in the Eucharist, Jesus personally sends each of us out to share his presence in the world. The word "Mass" actually means "sending" (*Missa* in Latin). The final movement of the Mass sends us out into the world to share Jesus with other people.

This is not easy. There are moments when sharing Jesus with other people in our daily routine can feel like an impossible mission to fulfill.

Yet, Jesus promised us help in fulfilling our mission. On the day of Ascension when Jesus raised his hands to bless his disciples, he promised them "power from on high" to fulfil the work he was sending them to do (Luke 24:49; see also Matthew 28:18-20; Mark 16:14-20). Through the Concluding Rites at the end of Mass, Jesus promises us his power to fulfill the work he is sending us to do in the world.

The blessing ensures us that Jesus' power will be with us as we go out from the church building and try to put our faith into action.

Some of the Christian deeds Jesus is sending us to do will seem inconvenient, annoying, or even impossible. On our own, they actually would be impossible. The blessing at the end of Mass teaches us that we do not have to rely on our own power and resources alone. The blessing promises us divine power to live our faith in heroic ways.

This is a time in the Mass to ask for divine assistance with living our vocation.

While the end of Mass is a moment of distractions, it is moment of tremendous significance. The blessing and dismissal at the end of Mass are a celebration of the goodness God sees within us, an affirmation of our personal mission in the world, and a promise of power from on high to live this mission in the world!

THANKS BE TO GOD

The People:
Thanks be to God.

On a warm June afternoon, I became quick friends with the pastor of a local non-denominational church. We met while waiting in the grill line of the cafeteria at St. Vincent's Hospital. The irony of our common lunch choice, greasy Philly cheesesteak sandwiches and fries, prior to visiting patients in the cardiac ICU was not lost on either of us. We decided to sit together for lunch and talk about ministry at our churches.

As Pastor Larry described to me his approach to Sunday worship, I immediately thought of some Catholic friends who had shared with me their desire for Mass to become more like a non-denominational service. Larry's church had a lively band with perfectly coordinated lighting effects. The worship space was filled with comfortable padded seats. Attendees felt like they were relaxing in a huge home theater. A trendy worship leader had the microphone on stage and delivered a memorable and entertaining sermon each week. Complimentary, fair-trade coffee was available for everyone before, during, and after the service.

I shared with Larry that some of my parishioners had suggested Catholic worship should be replaced with his style of worship. He smirked. What he said next shocked me.

"I know that I am successfully sharing the Christian faith when someone from my church tells me they desire a deeper form of worship than what we offer. Then I tell them they should check out the Catholic Mass." He continued, "my goal is to get people back into religion. Eventually though, they need a more intense form of worship if they really take Jesus' words seriously."

I put down my calorie-packed sandwich for a moment and sat back to think about what my new friend had just said. Larry picked up a salty French fry from his tray, leaned over the table, and pointed it at me. "The problem", he said, "is your people do not appreciate what they have at the Catholic Mass."

He was right. Many Catholics stray to other attractive forms of Sunday worship out of a sincere desire to encounter God. But they do not know what they are walking away from when they go elsewhere. Sadly, they could get more out of the Mass if someone actually taught them what to do and how to pray during the Mass.

Throughout this book, I've attempted to demonstrate how understanding the meaning of the structure, the words, and the gestures of the Mass can help us actively participate in the Mass and "get more out of it".

The final words of the Mass, words of gratitude, are the proper response when we have gone beyond a superficial experience of just going through the motions during Mass.

We give thanks that we have become part of something greater than ourselves through the Mass. It is a gift to share in the life of a community of faith that challenges us, supports us, and forces us to become more patient and less selfish.

We give thanks for the voice of God that has spoken to us through the Liturgy of the Word. It is a gift to hear the truth that pushes us beyond our own plans and preferences.

We give thanks that we have become more aware of people in need through the Mass. It is a gift to recognize that there is more to pursue in life than our own desires and comforts, as God calls us to serve others.

We give thanks for the greater knowledge of our own sinfulness that the Mass has revealed to us. It is a gift to know that Jesus believes we can improve, grow, change, and forgive if we cooperate with his grace and accept the potential he sees in us.

We give thanks for the real presence of Jesus in the Eucharist. It is a gift of immeasurable proportion to be united with the Son of God and to enter into a loving friendship with him that will last into eternity.

We give thanks for how Jesus has worked tangibly in our lives during the Mass through the ministry of the priest: his voice, his gestures, and his actions. It is a gift to encounter the perfect man, Jesus Christ, through the humble, imperfect humanity of an ordained minister.

The Mass takes us beyond ourselves. It teaches us that our existence is not just about us. The Mass challenges us to move beyond our desire to be entertained. The ritual of the Mass leads us away from the worship of our own ideas, plans, projects, and feelings to the worship of the God of the universe who has chosen us to be his beloved children.

There is always more we can get out of the Mass. However, the final words underline that the primary focus of our participation is not simply getting more out of it for ourselves. The Mass is about a relationship, a true friendship that involves both receiving and giving.

At Mass, we both give and receive love. We give ourselves to God. We offer our good works, our gifts, and our talents along with our brokenness, our fragility, and our sinfulness.

What we receive at Mass is ultimately an undeserved gift. What we get out of Mass is a relationship involving a love so deep, so beautiful, and so far beyond our comprehension that it moves us to kneel down in reverence and adoration, directs our minds to reflection and contemplation, and lifts up our hearts in gratitude to the God who knows us and loves us better than we do ourselves.

One of the greatest mistakes in the Christian life is to focus primarily on ourselves and to center our lives simply on whatever we consider most important in the moment. Our own preferences, plans, projects, and feelings can easily become the idol we worship and adore. The Mass frees us from this tragic fate as it draws us into community, not just with other Christians, but with the three persons of the Most Holy Trinity.

Thanks be to God for that!

Works Cited

[1] Pope Benedict XVI, *Homily at the Eucharistic Celebration on the Occasion of the 150th Anniversary of the Apparitions of the Blessed Virgin Mary*, September 14, 2008. Available online at: http://w2.vatican.va/content/benedict-xvi/en/homilies/2008/documents/hf_ben-xvi_hom_20080914_lourdes-apparizioni.html. Accessed August 28, 2020.

[2] *The General Instruction of the Roman Missal* (Washington DC: USCCB Communications, 2011), #45, 54. Hereafter: GIRM.

[3] Vatican II, *Dogmatic Constitution on Divine Revelation: Dei Verbum* (November 18, 1965), #21. Available online at: http://www.vatican.va/archive/hist_councils/ii_vatican_council/documents/vat-ii_const_19651118_dei-verbum_en.html Accessed: August 28, 2020.

[4] See the research of Felix Just on this topic. Available online at "The Catholic Lectionary Website": https://catholic-resources.org/Lectionary/Statistics.htm. Accessed August 20, 2020.

[5] See *Catechism of the Catholic Church* (Vatican City: Libreria Editrice Vaticana, 1997), #1156. Hereafter CCC. Available online at: http://www.vatican.va/archive/ENG0015/_INDEX.HTM For the original citation from St. Augustine (*Enarratio in Psalmos* 72, 1) see *The Companion to the Catechism of the Catholic Church* (San Francisco: Ignatius Press, 1994), 430-431. See also GIRM #39.

[6] Paul Turner, *At the Supper of the Lamb: A Pastoral and Theological Commentary on the Mass* (Chicago: Liturgy Training Publications, 2011), 32.

[7] See for example, Matthias Mehl, Simine Vazire, Nairán Ramírez-Esparza, Richard Slatcher, James Pennebaker, "Are Women Really More Talkative Than Men?" in *Science* 317(5834):82, August 2007.

[8] John Edward Bowden (editor), *The Spirit of the Curé of Ars* (London: Burns, Lambert, and Oates, 1865), 62.

[9] Cornell University Legacy Project, "Worry Wastes Your Life", available online at: http://legacyproject.human.cornell.edu/2013/04/11/worry-wastes-your-life-2/ Accessed August 28, 2020. See also, Karen Pillemer, *30 Lessons for Living: Tried and True Advice from the Wisest Americans* (New York: PLUME Books, 2011), 217-226.

[10] Josh Linkner, "Don't Waste Your Time Worrying About What's Unlikely to Come True" available online at: https://www.forbes.com/sites/joshlinkner/2015/10/12/the-math-of-worrying/#2fd79f1316ae Accessed August 28, 2020.

[11] Mary Paula McCarthy and Mary Grace McCormack (editors), *Golden Counsels of Saint Francis de Sales*, transl. Peronne Marie Thibert (St. Louis: Monastery of the Visitation, 2006), 7.

[12] GIRM #69.

[13] See Christopher Carstens and Douglas Martis, *Encountering Christ in the Words of the Mass* (Chicago: Liturgy Training Publications, 2011), 162.

[14] St. Cyprian, *Epistle 62: "On the Sacrament of the Cup of the Lord"*, 13. Available online at: http://www.newadvent.org/fathers/050662.htm. Accessed August 29, 2020.

[15] St. Athanasius, *De incarnatione*, 54, 3: PG 25, 192B. See CCC #460.

[16] GIRM #75.

[17] GIRM #76.

[18] GIRM #79. CCC #1352.

[19] CCC #1045.

[20] CCC #1024.

[21] See CCC #349, 1046.

[22] CCC #1352.

[23] CCC #1326.

[24] See "host" in Paul J. Achtemeier (editor), *HarperCollins Bible Dictionary* (San Francisco: HarperCollins, 1991), 441. Hereafter HCBD.

[25] CCC #559.

[26] CCC #1105, 1353.

[27] See, for example, CCC #1373-1381, 1413.

[28] GIRM #79.

[29] CCC #1362-1367.

[30] CCC #662, 666.

[31] See, for example, Leviticus 1-5.

[32] See, for example, the description of Leviticus 22:17-25.

[33] GIRM #79. CCC #1367.

[34] CCC #1368.

[35] CCC #1369.

[36] Elisabeth Kübler-Ross, *On Death and Dying* (New York: Macmillan Publishing, 1969), 21-37, 245-255.

[37] See "Preface I for the Dead" in *The Roman Missal*.

[38] CCC #1689, emphasis added.

[39] CCC #531-534.

[40] See George Weigel, *Witness to Hope: The Biography of Pope John Paul II* (New York: HarperCollins, 2001), 26-31, 68-69.

[41] Saint Cyprian, *Treatise on the Lord's Prayer* (Cap. 1-3: CSEL 3, 267-268). See Tuesday, 1st Week of Lent, Office of Readings.

[42] See, for example: Matthew 8:16-17, 28-34; 9:32-33; 10:1; 12:22-32; 15:21-28; 17:14-21; Mark 1:21-28, 32-34; 5:1-20; 9:14-29; Luke 4:31-37, 41; 8:26-39; 9:37-43; 11:14-23.

[43] See "Satan" in Paul J. Achtemeier (editor), HCBD, 974-975.

[44] See "devil" in Paul J. Achtemeier (editor), HCBD, 241.

[45] GIRM #82.

[46] Paul Turner, *At the Supper of the Lamb*, 135.

[47] CCC #1369.

[48] GIRM #83.

[49] See Christopher Carstens and Douglas Martis, *Encountering Christ in the Words of the Mass*, 216-218.

[50] CCC #608, 613-614. See 1 Peter 1:18-21.

[51] Mario Vargas Llosa, *The Temptation of the Impossible: Victor Hugo and Les Misérables*, transl. John King (Princeton: Princeton University Press, 2007), 63-64.

[52] GIRM #84.

[53] CCC #1331, 1405, 2837.

[54] CCC #1331, 1392, 1517, 1524-1525.

[55] Walter Ciszek, *He Leadeth Me* (San Francisco: Ignatius Press, 1995), 126-127.

[56] GIRM #89.

ACKNOWLEDGEMENTS

I extend my thanks to all who encouraged me in this project.

To the students at The University of Toledo and Corpus Christi University Parish, for their probing questions and unfiltered remarks about the Mass that pushed me more deeply into the Sacred Mysteries.

To Beth Church, for serving as a most helpful copy editor, patiently polishing my prose.

To John Wood and Michael Smith, for being the first to read through a draft, and providing important suggestions.

To the many professors and mentors who deepened my understanding of the Mass over the years. They are too numerous to list. Some whose courses left the most lasting impression include: José Granados, DCJM, Scott Hahn, Alexandra Diriart, CSJ, Kurt Belsole, OSB, Dan Pattee, TOR, and Cesare Giraudo, SJ. While these experts have a wide range of theological backgrounds and outlooks, each contributed to my ongoing understanding of the Sacred Liturgy and motivated me to study further.

To my parishioners at various parishes in the Diocese of Toledo, for sharing their lives with me through their prayerful participation in the Eucharist.

To the many priests from the Diocese of Toledo, both living and deceased, whose presence at the altar inspired me to answer God's call to priesthood.

To my parents, for taking me to Mass as a kid and teaching, by example, that the Mass is a tremendous gift. This book is dedicated to you.

P.A.S.

Sylvania, Ohio

January 2021

ABOUT THE AUTHOR

Philip A. Smith

Father Philip Smith is a priest of the Diocese of Toledo, Ohio. He earned a BA in catechetics, theology, and philosophy from Franciscan University of Steubenville. He completed graduate degrees at the Pontifical Gregorian University and the Pontifical John Paul II Institute for Studies on Marriage and Family in Rome. He has ministered at several parishes in the Diocese of Toledo, including five years at Corpus Christi University Parish at The University of Toledo where he was also Director of the Christian Leadership Program. He currently serves as Pastor of a parish and Director of the Office for Diocesan Priestly Vocations.